PENGUIN BOOKS
THE PLEASURES AND SORROWS OF WORK

'A winning mixture of razor-sharp intellect and self-deprecating humour' *GQ*

'Distinctive and personable. If this thoughtful book has proved one thing it is that work continues to fascinate and frustrate in equal measure' *Financial Times*

'A luminous photo-essay from a consistently fresh and noble writer' *Kirkus*

'The pleasure of this book, as with all of de Botton's writings, is that his seriousness is deployed without heaviness. He has a gift for properly noticing things, and a capacity to illuminate them with enticing prose that blends erudition, witty allusion and a sense of wonder' *Canberra Times*

'A pilgrimage through the late-industrial world . . . an intricate, often melancholic, at times wry and occasionally outraged bird's-eye view of our muddled and paradoxical civilization' *Sydney Morning Herald*

'The minute details of how we work – fishing tuna, inventing biscuits, painting trees – are fascinating' *Inquire*

'A provocative thinker who truly wants to improve people's lives' *Metro*

'De Botton is a gifted writer . . . There is something undoubtedly refreshing in a book which doesn't rush to judgement but has the courage simply to help readers do the work of thinking for themselves' *Waterstone's Books Quarterly*

Alain de Botton is the author of bestselling books including *The Consolations of Philosophy*, *The Art of Travel*, *How Proust Can Change Your Life* and *Essays in Love*. His work has been published in twenty-five countries. Born in 1969, he lives in London, where he helped to set up The School of Life (www.theschooloflife.com). For further information, see www.alaindebotton.com.

The Pleasures and Sorrows of Work
Alain de Botton

PENGUIN BOOKS

PENGUIN BOOKS

Published by the Penguin Group
Penguin Books Ltd, 80 Strand, London WC2R 0RL, England
Penguin Group (USA), Inc., 375 Hudson Street, New York, New York 10014, USA
Penguin Group (Canada), 90 Eglinton Avenue East, Suite 700, Toronto, Ontario, Canada M4P 2Y3
(a division of Pearson Penguin Canada Inc.)
Penguin Ireland, 25 St Stephen's Green, Dublin 2, Ireland (a division of Penguin Books Ltd)
Penguin Group (Australia), 250 Camberwell Road,
Camberwell, Victoria 3124, Australia (a division of Pearson Australia Group Pty Ltd)
Penguin Books India Pvt Ltd, 11 Community Centre,
Panchsheel Park, New Delhi – 110 017, India
Penguin Group (NZ), 67 Apollo Drive, Rosedale, North Shore 0632, New Zealand
(a division of Pearson New Zealand Ltd)
Penguin Books (South Africa) (Pty) Ltd, 24 Sturdee Avenue,
Rosebank, Johannesburg 2196, South Africa

Penguin Books Ltd, Registered Offices: 80 Strand, London WC2R 0RL, England

www.penguin.com

First published by Hamish Hamilton 2009
Published in Penguin Books 2010
2

Copyright © Alain de Botton, 2009
Photographs (excepting those otherwise attributed on page 328) © Richard Baker, 2009
All rights reserved

The moral right of the author has been asserted

Typeset by Thomas Manss & Company
Printed and bound in China

ISBN: 978-0-141-02791-3

for Samuel

House-building, measuring, sawing the boards,
Blacksmithing, glass-blowing, nail-making, coopering,
    tin-roofing, shingle-dressing,
Ship-joining, dock-building, fish-curing, flagging of sidewalks
    by flaggers,
The pump, the pile-driver, the great derrick, the coal-kiln
    and brick-kiln,
Coal-mines and all that is down there, the lamps in the darkness,
    echoes, songs, what meditations...

    – from Walt Whitman, 'A Song for Occupations'

Contents

I

Cargo Ship Spotting

1.

Imagine a journey across one of the great cities of the modern world. Take London on a particularly grey Monday at the end of October. Fly over its distribution centres, reservoirs, parks and mortuaries. Consider its criminals and South Korean tourists. See the sandwich-making plant at Park Royal, the airline contract-catering facility in Hounslow, the DHL delivery depot in Battersea, the Gulfstreams at City airport and the cleaning trolleys in the Holiday Inn Express on Smuggler's Way. Listen to the screaming in the refectory of Southwark Park primary school and the silenced guns at the Imperial War Museum. Think of driving instructors, meter readers and hesitant adulterers. Stand in the maternity ward of St Mary's Hospital. Watch Aashritha, three and a half months too early for existence, enmeshed in tubes, sleeping in a plastic box manufactured in the Swiss Canton of Obwalden. Look into the State Room on the west side of Buckingham Palace. Admire the Queen, having lunch with two hundred disabled athletes, then over coffee, making a speech in praise of determination. In Parliament, follow the government minister introducing a bill regulating the height of electrical sockets in public buildings. Consider the trustees of the National Gallery voting to acquire a painting by the eighteenth-century Italian artist Giovanni Panini. Scan the faces of the prospective Father Christmases being interviewed in the basement of Selfridges in Oxford Street and wonder at the diction of the Hungarian psychoanalyst delivering a lecture on paranoia and breastfeeding at the Freud Museum in Hampstead.

Meanwhile, at the capital's eastern edges, another event is occuring which will leave no trace in the public mind or attract attention from anyone beyond its immediate participants, but which is no less worthy of record for that. *The Goddess of the Sea* is making her way to the Port of London from Asia. Built a decade earlier by Mitsubishi Heavy Industries in Nagasaki, she is 390 metres long, painted orange and grey and wears her name defiantly, for she makes little attempt to evoke any of the qualities of grace and beauty for which goddesses are traditionally famed, being instead squat and 80,000 tonnes in weight, with a stern that bulges like an overstuffed cushion and a hold stacked high with more than a thousand variously-coloured steel containers full of cargo, whose origins range from the factories of the Kobe corridor to the groves of the Atlas Mountains.

This leviathan is headed not for the better-known bits of the river, where tourists buy ice-creams to the smell of diesel engines, but to a place where the waters are coloured a dirty brown and the banks are gnawed by jetties and warehouses – an industrial zone which few of the capital's inhabitants penetrate, though the ordered running of their lives and, not least, their supplies of Tango fizzy orange and cement aggregate depend on its complex operations.

Our ship reached the English Channel late the previous evening and followed the arc of the Kent coastline to a point a few miles north of Margate, where, at dawn, she began the final phase of her journey up the lower Thames, a haunted-looking setting evocative both of the primeval past and of a dystopian future, a place where one half expects that a brontosaurus might emerge from behind the shell of a burnt-out car factory.

The river's ostensibly generous width in fact offers but a single, narrow navigable channel. Used to having hundreds of metres of water to play with, the ship now advances gingerly, like a proud creature of the wild confined to a zoo enclosure, her sonar letting out a steady sequence of coy beeps. Up on the bridge, the Malaysian captain scans a nautical chart, which delineates every underwater

ridge and bank from Canvey Island to Richmond, while the surrounding landscape, even where it is densest with monuments and civic buildings, looks like the 'terra incognita' marked on the charts of early explorers. On either side of the ship, the river swirls with plastic bottles, feathers, cork, sea-smoothed planks, felt-tip pens and faded toys.

The Goddess docks at Tilbury container terminal at just after eleven. Given the trials she has undergone, she might have expected to be met by a minor dignitary or a choir singing 'Exultate, jubilate'. But there is a welcome only from a foreman, who hands a Filipino crew member a sheaf of customs forms and disappears without asking what dawn looked like over the Malacca Straits or whether there were porpoises off Sri Lanka.

The ship's course alone is impressive. Three weeks earlier she set off from Yokohama and since then she has called in at Yokkaichi, Shenzhen, Mumbai, Istanbul, Casablanca and Rotterdam. Only days before, as a dull rain fell on the sheds of Tilbury, she began her ascent up the Red Sea under a relentless sun, circled by a family of storks from Djibouti. The steel cranes now moving over her hull break up a miscellaneous cargo of fan ovens, running shoes, calculators, fluorescent bulbs, cashew nuts and vividly coloured toy animals. Her boxes of Moroccan lemons will end up on the shelves of central London shops by evening. There will be new television sets in York at dawn.

Not that many consumers care to dwell on where their fruit has come from, much less where their shirts have been made or who fashioned the rings which connect their shower hose to the basin. The origins and travels of our purchases remain matters of indifference, although – to the more imaginative at least – a slight dampness at the bottom of a carton, or an obscure code printed along

a computer cable, may hint at processes of manufacture and transport nobler and more mysterious, more worthy of wonder and study, than the very goods themselves

2.

The Goddess of the Sea is only one of dozens of ships making their way up the Thames on this October day. A Finnish vessel arrives from the Baltic Sea, laden with rolls of paper the width of railway tunnels, destined to feed the chattering presses of Wapping and West Ferry. A freighter sits low in the water next to Tilbury power station, weighed down by 5,000 tonnes of Colombian coal – enough fuel to fire the kettles and hairdryers of eastern England until the New Year.

At a quayside, a car transporter opens its heavy-jawed cargo doors to emit three thousand family saloons which have spent twenty days at sea since leaving their assembly plant at Ulsan, on the Korean peninsula. These near-identical Hyundai Amicas, smelling of newly minted plastic and synthetic carpet, will bear witness to sandwich lunches and arguments, love-making and motorway songs. They will be driven to beauty spots and left to gather leaves in school car parks. A few will kill their owners. To peer inside these untouched vehicles, their seats wrapped in brown paper printed with elegant and cryptic Korean entreaties, is to have a feeling of intruding on an innocence more normally associated with the slumber of new-borns.

But the port shows little interest in lyrical associations. Around Tilbury, the shipping companies present their services bluntly from within their smoked-glass headquarters. To reassure and seduce their clients, they imply that their vessels' journeys – even those which involve rounding the Cape of Good Hope in winter, or shouldering thirty jet engines across the Pacific – have all the mundanity of a ride between adjoining stations on an Underground line.

Nevertheless, no quayside can ever appear entirely banal, because people will always be miniscule compared to the great oceans and the mention of faraway ports will hence always bear a confused promise of lives unfolding there which may be more vivid than the ones we know here, a romantic charge clinging to names like Yokohama, Alexandria and Tunis – places which in reality cannot be exempt from tedium and compromise, but which are distant enough to support for a time certain confused daydreams of happiness.

3.

In truth, the ships' destination is not a single, cohesive port but rather a loose conjunction of terminals and factories untidily lining a stretch of the Thames between Gravesend and the Woolwich ferry. It is here that vessels slip in continuously, during humid summers and fog-bound winters, night and day, to deliver the bulk of London's gravel and its reinforced steel, its soya beans and coal, its milk and its paper pulp, the sugar cane for its biscuits and the hydrocarbons for its generators – an area as noteworthy as any of the museums of the city, but about which the guidebooks are always silent.

Numerous factories are situated on the very bank of the river, close enough to scoop or suck raw materials directly from the holds of ships, and are at work producing some of the less celebrated ingredients behind the smooth functioning of our utilitarian civilisation: the polyols added to toothpaste to help it retain its moisture, the citric acid used to stabilise laundry detergent, the isoglucose to sweeten cereal, the glyceryl tristearate to make soap and the xanthan gum to ensure the viscosity of gravy.

In charge of these processes are engineers who have successfully stamped out their natural laziness to master the austere dilemmas

of chemistry and physics, people who may have spent twenty years specialising in the storage of flammable solvents or the reaction of wood pulp to water vapour – and in their leisure time, leaf through the *Hazardous Cargo Bulletin*, the world's only monthly magazine dedicated to the safe handling and transport of oils and chemicals.

However inhuman the facilities of the port might seem in scale, it is in the end only our own personal and prosaic appetites that have created them. A river-side factory, with tubes like a hydra's tentacles snaking around its midriff and crowned by a chimney wheezing orange smoke, is responsible for nothing more sinister or esoteric than the manufacture of cheddar biscuits. A tanker has crossed the muddy-brown North Sea from Rotterdam carrying carbon dioxide with which to make bubbles for children's lemonade. The steely grey box of the Kimberly-Clark factory at Northfleet, eight storeys high and large enough to shelter an aircraft carrier, is turning out cartons of two-ply toilet roll. It is our collective tastes for sweets and nuts, drinks and tissues which has summoned ships from distant continents and thrown up industrial towers vying with the dome of St Paul's.

So arcane are the operations around the port that no single person could ever hope to grasp more than a fragment of their totality. A ship's captain may enjoy superlative command over the contours of the lower Thames, but no sooner has his vessel docked than he will be relegated to the status of an apprentice observer of the business of jetty engineering and the long-term refrigeration of citrus fruit – his jurisdiction ending as abruptly as the authority of his nautical chart.

However, any sadness we might feel about the demise of the generalist can be offset by the recognition that our age offers us access to unimpeachable masters of specific trades, for example, the storage of bitumen or the construction of ship-loading conveyors

– in itself as comforting as the thought that there exist professors of medicine concentrated solely on the workings of human liver enzymes, or that at any time, several hundred scholars across the world are investigating nothing but the later Merovingian period of Frankish history, writing up their findings for the *Zeitschrift für Archäologie des Mittelalters*, an academic journal published by the humanities department at the University of Tübingen.

The drift toward specialisation exists at the mechanical level too. The port area is filled with machines unavailable to the general public, which have none of the flexibility, but then again none of the dilettantish weaknesses, of generic conveyances like lorries and vans. They resemble peculiar-looking animals whose isolated habitats have rewarded the emergence of strange talents – the ability to suck beetles out of mud through one's nose, for instance, or to hang upside down above an underground river – while forgiving a lack of more pedestrian skills. The R30XM2 lift-truck built by the Hyster Corporation of Cleveland, Ohio, may have a top speed of just five kilometres an hour, but in the restricted context of a warehouse, it skims gracefully along concrete floors and exhibits a balletic agility in extricating rolls of paper from the top shelves on either side of a tight aisle.

It seems natural to admire the patience and nerves of those who have put up the money to build these limbs of industry, for example, the two hundred and fifty million dollars required merely to dip the keel of a trans-Pacific container ship into the water. The investors know that there is nothing implausible or hubristic in their appropriating the life savings of a nation's postmen or nurses and then betting those sums on the financing of warehouses in Panama and back offices in Hamburg. They can let their funds disappear out of sight for a decade or more, leave them in the hands of captains

and first officers, allow them to cross the Tropics of Capricorn and Cancer, sail the Long Island Sound and the Ionian Sea, dock in the container ports of Aden and Tangiers, confident that their investment will eventually sluice back to them swollen with the rewards of patience and application. They know that their outlay is in truth a form of prudence and incomparably less dangerous than leaving the money under the bed, to the eventual impoverishment and ruination of all.

4.

Why, then, endowed as they are with both practical importance and emotional resonance, do the cargo ships and port facilities go unnoticed, except by those immediately involved in their operations?

It is not just because they are hard to locate and forbiddingly signposted. Some of Venice's churches are similarly secreted away but nonetheless prodigally visited. What renders the ships and ports invisible is an unwarranted prejudice which deems it peculiar to express overly powerful feelings of admiration towards a gas tanker or a paper mill – or indeed towards almost any aspect of the labouring world.

Yet not everyone has been dissuaded. At the end of a pier in Gravesend, five men are standing together in the rain. They are dressed in waterproof plastic jackets and heavy-soled boots. They are silent and intent, looking out at the mist-cloaked river. They are tracking a shape, which they know from their timetables to be the *Grande Nigeria*. They also know that she is bound for Lagos, that her hold is filled with Ford parts for the African market, that she is powered by two Sulzer 900 diesel engines and that she measures 214 metres from stem to stern.

There is no practical reason for their scrutiny. They are not in charge of preparing her berth for its next occupant or, like the staff at the nearby control tower, assigning her a shipping lane for the journey out to the North Sea. They wish only to admire her and note her passage. They bring to the study of harbour life a devotion more often witnessed in relation to art, their behaviour implying a belief that creativity and intelligence can be as present in the transport of axles around the tip of the western Sahara as they are in the use of an impasto in a female nude. Yet how fickle museum-goers seem by comparison, with their impatient interest in cafeterias, their susceptibility to gift shops, their readiness to avail themselves of benches. How seldom has a man spent two hours in a rain-storm in front of *Hendrickje Bathing* with only a thermos of coffee for sustenance.

Admittedly, the ship spotters do not respond to the objects of their enthusiasm with particular imagination. They traffic in statistics. Their energies are focused on logging dates and shipping speeds, recording turbine numbers and shaft lengths. They behave like a man who has fallen deeply in love and asks his companion if he might act on his emotions by measuring the distance between her elbow and her shoulder blade. But in converting a passion into a set of facts, the spotters are at least following a pattern with an established pedigree, most noticeable in academia, where an art historian, on being stirred to tears by the tenderness and serenity he detects in a work by a fourteenth-century Florentine painter, may end up writing a monograph, as irreproachable as it is bloodless, on the history of paint manufacture in the age of Giotto. It seems easier to respond to our enthusiasms by trading in facts than by investigating the more naive question of how and why we have been moved.

But whatever their inarticulacies, the ship-spotters are at least appropriately alive to some of the most astonishing aspects of our time. They know what it is about our world that would detain a Martian or a child. They take pleasure in sensing their smallness and ignorance next to the expansive intelligence of the modern collective mind. Standing beside a docked ship, their heads thrown back to gaze at its steel turrets disappearing into the sky, they enter into a state of silent, satisfied wonder, like pilgrims before the buttresses of Chartres.

Nor are they ashamed to seem eccentric when their curiosity demands it. They crouch low to catch sight of ships' propellers. They fall asleep thinking of where in the ocean a particular tanker might be. Their concentration recalls that of a small child who comes to a halt in the centre of a crowded shopping street and, while passers-by swerve to avoid her, bends down to examine, with the care of a biblical scholar poring over the pages of a vellum-bound book, a piece of chewing gum impressed on the pavement, or the closing mechanism of her coat pocket. They are like children, too, in their upending of conventional ideas of what might constitute a good job, always valuing a profession's intrinsic interest over its relative material benefit, judging with particular favour the post of crane operator at a container terminal because of the vantage point it offers over ships and quaysides, just as a child might aspire to drive a train because of the seductive hiss of the carriage's hydraulic doors, or to run a post office based on the satisfaction of adhering airmail labels onto puffy envelopes.

The ship-spotters' pastime harks back to the habits of premodern travellers, who, upon arriving in a new country, were apt to express particular curiosity about its granaries, aqueducts, harbours and workshops, feeling that the observation of work could be as stimulating as anything on a stage or chapel wall – a relief from a contemporary view which tightly associates tourism with play and therefore steers us away from an interest in aluminium foundries and sewage treatment plants in favour of the trumpeted pleasures of musicals and waxwork museums.

The men down by the river have broken free of such expectations, they freely express their concern for the movement of freight and the thunder of conveyor belts. Whereas an ordinary onlooker might, from their pier, see nothing more than three lorries pulling out of a factory yard, *they* have learnt to recognise the continuing odyssey of a shipment of Brazilian cane, brought over on the freighter *Valeria* and now turned into sugar, leaving the Tate and Lyle refinery at Silvertown bound for a Derby establishment involved in raisin cakes. Their satisfactions are akin to those of an ornithologist who, on glimpsing through a pair of binoculars a creature which most people would dismiss as just another blue-grey bird, knows to celebrate the spring's first sighting of a *phylloscopus trochilus*, resting at the close of its four-thousand-mile journey from its winter habitat in the marshlands of the Ivory Coast.

5.

How ignorant most of us are by contrast, surrounded by machines and processes of which we have only the loosest grasp; we who know nothing about gantry cranes and iron-ore bulk carriers, who register the economy only as a set of numbers, who have avoided close study of switch gears and wheat storage and spare ourselves closer acquaintance with the manufacturing protocols for tensile steel cable. How much we might learn from the men at the end of a pier on the edges of London.

They inspired this book, which the author hopes might function a little like one of those eighteenth-century cityscapes which show us people at work from the quayside to the temple, the parliament to the counting house, panoramas like those of Canaletto in which, within a single giant frame, one can witness dockers unloading crates, merchants bargaining in the main square, bakers before their ovens, women sewing at their windows and councils of ministers assembled in a palace – inclusive scenes which serve to remind us of the place which work accords each of us within the human hive.

I was inspired by the men at the pier to attempt a hymn to the intelligence, peculiarity, beauty and horror of the modern work-place and, not least, its extraordinary claim to be able to provide us, alongside love, with the principal source of life's meaning.

II

Logistics

i: A logistics hub

1.

Two centuries ago, our forebears would have known the precise history and origin of nearly every one of the limited number of things they ate and owned, as well as of the people and tools involved in their production. They were acquainted with the pig, the carpenter, the weaver, the loom and the dairymaid. The range of items available for purchase may have grown exponentially since then, but our understanding of their genesis has diminished almost to the point of obscurity. We are now as imaginatively disconnected from the manufacture and distribution of our goods as we are practically in reach of them, a process of alienation which has stripped us of myriad opportunities for wonder, gratitude and guilt.

Critical to both our imaginative impoverishment and our practical enrichment is the field of endeavour known as logistics, a name rooted in the Ancient Greek military figure of the *logistikos* or quartermaster, who was once responsible for supplying an army with food and weaponry. Today the term is used to refer collectively to the arts of warehousing, inventory, packaging and transport, an industry which counts among its greatest achievements the 'cool corridor' between Africa and Europe down which cut-flowers and vegetables travel, the FedEx hub in Memphis, Tennessee, and the development of the corrugated fibreboard box.

2.

In the centre of England, a few miles southwest of the River Avon, near King James I's palace at Holdenby House, stands a group of twenty-five imposing grey warehouses – of a sort common to the landscapes of all industrialised nations, the kind which line

ring-roads and airports, yet rarely explain their purpose to onlookers, mutely repelling the curiosity or outrage they can generate. The warehouses together make up one of the largest and most technologically advanced logistics parks in Europe. Positioned beside three central arteries, the M1, M6 and A5, they are within a four-hour drive of 80 percent of the United Kingdom's population, and every week, largely at night, they handle a significant share of its supply of building materials, stationery, food, furniture and computers.

Despite their importance, the warehouses have no desire to advertise themselves to the public. They are spread out across a site of determined blandness marked by gentle gradients, ornamental trees and expanses of preternaturally green grass. They have no interest in the problems and possibilities of architecture. They care only for size. One looks up at their cathedral-like ceilings and finds, instead of angels, workaday, economical spans of steel punctuated by fluorescent strips, which guide the onlooker's eyes back to rows of symmetrical shelving and the hurried motions of forklift trucks. That the logistics hub has been allowed to assume this stark and monolithic appearance signals our confusion about how much it matters what is in front of our eyes. We accept that museums can devote fortunes to acquiring tender Early Netherlandish devotional paintings no larger than hardback books, but we see nothing foolhardy in casually surrendering large strips of the planet to the impatient interests of men from Jones Lange Lasalle, out of a curious reluctance to concede that we may in the end be as inwardly affected by the sight of five square kilometres of warehouse space incised into the fields of Northamptonshire as by the benevolent gaze of a twenty-centimetre Madonna from the workshop of Rogier van der Weyden.

Yet it would be foolish to describe the logistics hub as merely ugly, for it has the horrifying, soulless, immaculate beauty characteristic of many of the workplaces of the modern world.

At the top of a slope on the perimeter of the site, overlooking six lanes of motorway, is a diner frequented by lorry drivers who have either just unloaded or are waiting to pick up their cargo. Anyone nursing a disappointment with domestic life would find relief in this tiled, brightly lit cafeteria with its smells of fries and petrol, for it has the reassuring feel of a place where everyone is just passing through – and which therefore has none of the close-knit or convivial atmosphere which could cast a humiliating light on one's own alienation. It suggests itself as an ideal location for Christmas lunch for those let down by their families. Patrons can tour the aisles of a generous self-service buffet, combine fish pie with deep-pan pizza or hamburger with curry, without needing to apologise for the size or eccentricity of their selections and silently take a seat at one of the yellow plastic tables which look out onto the stream of ruby-red tail lamps outside.

Roadworks are common on these stretches of motorway and serve to slow the traffic almost to a standstill, allowing one to follow the incremental progress of Skania and Iveco lorries packed with industrial quantities of items which one normally contemplates only on a domestic scale: chocolate bars, cereal, bottled water, mattresses and margarine all inching their way northwards in the darkness. The view has some of the consoling qualities of a river, whose constant play of shadow and current may lift an observer out of a mood of stagnation. It is life itself rolling past, in its most heedless, savage, selfish manifestations, endowed with the same impassive will which impels the spread of bacteria and jungle flora.

3.

The single-mindedness of the goings-on in the logistics park are most transparent at night, when the appearance of the moon questions the significance of efficient courier services from an inter-planetary viewpoint, as does – from the perspective of eternity – a slender church spire built in the late fourteenth century, visible as a pitch-black arrow on the far side of the motorway.

Nightfall used to be the time when members of our species would acknowledge their physical limitations and huddle together to miti-gate their fear of ghosts and witches. The logistics hub, however, makes few concessions to human frailty, the spirit world or the primacy of natural rhythms. Floodlights come on to compensate for the sun's retreat, bathing the area in the nocturnal orange glow famil-iar from airports and military installations. Workers are dropped off by bus at a central reception area and clock in before seven. On a site which was once fields of barley and wheat, warehouses now await shipments of lawn mowers, work-out benches and barbecue sets. Passing motorists, seeing the glare from the forecourts through the fog, might be forgiven for wondering what ungodly preparations could be in train at this hour.

The work that unfolds here casts most of us who unknowingly benefit from it in a passive role. We will lie in bed, now and then shifting from one side to the other, our mouths defencelessly agape, while a fleet of lorries is loaded up with the lion's share of the morn-ing's semi-skimmed milk for northern England. To witness the park's activities in the darkness is to recall those moments in child-hood when we woke up after midnight and heard footsteps and other noises outside our bedroom door, the parental unloading of crockery, perhaps, or the rearrangement of furniture, and thereby derived a sense of the labours which underpinned the daytime order of our household.

4.

The largest warehouse in the logistics park belongs to a supermarket chain, which throughout the night receives dispatches from food suppliers and recombines them for onward delivery to stores across the country. The aisles of an average supermarket contain twenty thousand items, four thousand of which are chilled and need to be replaced every three days, while the other sixteen thousand require restocking within two weeks. There are fifty lorry bays running along the length of the building and vehicles arriving and departing at a rate of one every three minutes.

Inside, staff circulate between shelves, placing goods onto automated runways, which rush them to rows of steel cages lined up behind the loading bays, where they wait to be driven to a range of obscurely numbered destinations. 02093-30 refers to a cathedral town boasting a theatre and a brewery, a place which hosted a Parliamentarian army during the Civil War and retains several fine Georgian squares and which every morning, unnoticed by most of its residents, is visited by an articulated lorry from across the Pennine Hills, carrying in its hold parmesan cheese, red jelly, fishcakes and lamb cutlets.

Components of the national diet race around the building on conveyor belts high above the ground: thirty cartons of crisps for Northfleet, 1,200 chicken drumsticks for Hams Hall, sixty crates of lemonade for Elstree. Human beings, once segregated into dietary categories almost as strongly as by religious ones, into the peoples of rice or of wheat, of potatoes or of maize, now fill their stomachs with unthinking promiscuity.

Time is of the essence. At any given moment, half the contents of the warehouse are seventy-two hours away from being inedible, a prospect which prompts continuous struggles against the challenges of mould and geography. Clusters of tomatoes still attached to their vine, having ripened to maturity in fields near Palermo at the weekend, are exchanging the destiny seemingly assigned to them by nature to try to find buyers for themselves on the northern fringes of Scotland before Thursday.

Blind impatience is equally evident in the fruit section. Our ancestors might have delighted in the occasional handful of berries found on the underside of a bush in late summer, viewing them as a sign of the unexpected munificence of a divine creator, but we became modern when we gave up on awaiting sporadic gifts from above and sought to render any pleasing sensation immediately and repeatedly available.

It is early December and in a central aisle, twelve thousand blood-red strawberries wait in the semi-darkness. They flew in from California yesterday, crossing over the Arctic circle by moonlight, writing a trail of nitrogen oxide across a black and gold sky. The supermarket will never again let the shifting axis of the earth delay its audience's dietary satisfactions: strawberries journey in from Israel in midwinter, from Morocco in February, from Spain in spring, from Holland in early summer, from England in August and from the groves behind San Diego between September and Christmas. There is only ninety-six hours' leeway between the moment the strawberries are picked and the moment they start to cave in to attacks of grey mould. An improbable number of grown-ups have been forced to subordinate their sloth, to move pallets across sheds and wait in rumbling diesel lorries in traffic to bow to the exacting demands of soft plump fruit.

If only security concerns were not so paramount in the imagination of its owners, the warehouse would make a perfect tourist destination, for observing the movement of lorries and products in

the middle of the night induces a mood of distinctive tranquillity, it magically stills the demands of the ego and corrects any danger of looming too large in one's own imagination. That we are each surrounded by millions of other human beings remains a piece of inert and unevocative data, failing to dislodge us from a self-centered day-to-day perspective, until we take a look at a stack of ten thousand ham-and-mustard sandwiches, all wrapped in identical plastic casings, assembled in a factory in Hull, made out of the same flawless cottony-white bread, and due to be eaten over the coming two days by an extraordinary range of our fellow citizens which these sandwiches promptly urge us to make space for in our inwardly focused imaginations.

This gargantuan granary is evidence that we have become, after several thousand years of effort, in the industrialised world at least, the only animals to have wrested ourselves from an anxious search for the source of the next meal and therefore to have opened up new stretches of time – in which we can learn Swedish, master calculus and worry about the authenticity of our relationships, avoiding the compulsive and all-consuming dietary priorities under which still labour the emperor penguin and Arabian oryx.

Yet our world of abundance, with seas of wine and alps of bread, has hardly turned out to be the ebullient place dreamt of by our ancestors in the famine-stricken years of the Middle Ages. The brightest minds spend their working lives simplifying or accelerating functions of unreasonable banality. Engineers write theses on the velocities of scanning machines and consultants devote their careers to implementing minor economies in the movements of shelf-stackers and forklift operators. The alcohol-inspired fights that break out in market towns on Saturday evenings are predictable symptoms of fury at our incarceration. They are a reminder of the

price we pay for our daily submission at the altars of prudence and order – and of the rage that silently accumulates beneath a uniquely law-abiding and compliant surface.

5.

Dominating the eastern end of the warehouse is an encyclopedic selection of the inhabitants of the world's oceans. Stacked on shelves in the middle of the English countryside are mackerel icefish from Australia, red rock lobster from Mexico, hoki from New Zealand, Mahi Mahi from Ecuador and monkfish from Costa Rica.

To consider the expressions of these creatures, with their faces by turns noble, gauche, ugly, wise and terrifying, is to be pulled from our ordinary agenda and made to acknowledge man's co-proprietorship of the planet with some distinctive beings whom we have condemned to end their existence under rings of lemon because of no greater error on their part than the possession of a fleshy texture and a lack of small bones.

How did the fish find their way here? How did they die? Who made the packaging? And, more imaginatively, what might a painter discover in rendering a mackerel's skin or an engineer in examining a red rock lobster's claws? Implicit in these questions is a broader failure to appreciate the interest and incidental beauty of the working world.

I notice a shelf stacked deep with fresh tuna steaks. 'Caught by line in the Maldives' says the wrapper, a claim as concise and tantalising as an epitaph on a gravestone. That fish taken out of the water several continents away could in a matter of hours be here in a warehouse in Northamptonshire is evidence of nothing short of logistical genius, based on a complex interplay of technology, managerial discipline and legal and economic standardisation.

It is the almost conspiratorial silence regarding this achievement that intrigues and provokes me – and with time gives birth to a desire to seize hold of a fish and follow it, at a somewhat more leisurely pace, backwards into the sea. It might of course have been some other commodity: I might have traced a roll of sheet steel from a Bavarian car factory to the scrub of the Australian desert or a skein of cotton from a loom in Mexico to the irrigated fields of the lower Nile. The tuna's lessons, while played out in particularities, are nonetheless general ones about the value of swimming upstream in order to observe the forgotten odysseys of crates, to witness the secret life of warehouses and hence to mitigate the deadening, uniquely modern sense of dislocation between the things we so heedlessly consume in the run of our daily lives and their unknown origins and creators.

I decide that I will anchor my journey around images, for it is tangible details in which the logistical field seems to be most sorely lacking. Herewith follows, therefore, a photo essay whose sole ambition is to alter, if only for a second or two, some of the thought processes that might occur the next time one is confronted by an object that has been transported mysteriously and at an implausible speed halfway around the planet in the darkness.

It is impossible to follow fish without
an appetite for humiliation. No one
wants to open up to writers, who bring
in no money and are liable to cause
trouble. Even in an era of increased
political transparency, businesses remain
uninterested in acquiring observers.
Attempts to trace – let alone to witness or
photograph – how warm-water fish reach
our tables are liable to provoke within
the industry some of the same suspicion
which must have greeted enquiries into
the slave trade in the 1780s. I contact
fifteen seafood importing businesses.
Three of them have the same sculpture of
a marlin in the lobby. All refuse to discuss
the details of their logistical networks.

There seems no alternative but to head to the Indian Ocean, hoping to pick up leads on the ground. In Male, the capital of the Maldives, the photographer and I check in to the Relax Inn, whose titular command we find ourselves unable to obey. For the first five days, we encounter nothing but dead ends. To kill time between fruitless appointments, we wander the city, visiting patriotic monuments and mosques. Behind the Seagull Café, we discover a small cemetery dedicated to dead holidaymakers, most of them from Norway, Germany and England. They are commemorated here not because they were unwanted back home, but because their relatives wished for them to spend their afterlives in soil more congenial than that found in their frozen, fog-bound homelands. The park honours not only those who managed to die here but also an equally large contingent who sorely wished to do so but in the end succumbed elsewhere, perhaps claimed by one of the many viruses which haunt the rain-sodden European plains in midwinter.

Our fortunes change when, after a discussion with a well-connected hairdresser, we secure an appointment with no less a figure than Abdulla Naseer, the Minister for Fish, newly returned from an official visit to the United Nations. Wearing a pair of crocodile shoes, the minister greets us with gravitas, having a lucid awareness of his power, not just over the lives of fish, but of their captors too. After patiently listening to our story, he shouts a few orders to his subordinates in the next room, then offers to introduce us both to a tuna exporter and a group of fishermen in the northern islands. On our way out, he hands us a set of his business cards, allowing us to flash them at anyone who might cause us trouble on our peregrinations around his heavily policed island fiefdom. Unsure of how to pitch my gratitude, I suggest we have tea the next time he is in London.

We travel to an almost perfectly round kilometre long coral island, in the second most northerly atoll of the Maldivian chain. From the air, it is easy to mistake the place for a tourist resort, though from close up, it is lacking the requisite water villas, spas and couples from Baden-Württemberg renewing their marriage vows. There are only basic breeze-block huts, emergency water tanks donated by UNICEF, flies, a two-room school funded by a Saudi Arabian mosque and a single shop. We are informed on arrival that our fishermen have been stranded at sea by a broken engine. So we spend three inconceivably long days waiting in a boiling tin hut fitted out with two camp beds and an en suite tap, and reflect on the life of beetles and the sadness of small islands. In temperatures which reach 35 degrees centigrade in the shade, we often squat under a tree on the main patch of waste ground, watched over by President Maumoon Abdul Gayoom of the Maldives, the dictator, poet and Islamist whose portrait stands sentinel, by law, on every one of the country's two hundred inhabited islands – and who bears an uncanny physical resemblance to my late father.

At mealtimes, the locals disappear into their homes to fry up a medley of fish, coconut and onions, but as we lack the requisite culinary equipment, we come to rely extensively on the stock of the local shop – whose owner also becomes our only friend, it being hard to find kindred spirits in small communities. We have chocolate biscuits for breakfast, tinned tomatoes and mayonnaise for lunch and ketchup and sweetcorn for supper.

At last, the engine is fixed and we head out to sea. The fishing boat is under the command of captain Ibrahim Rasheed, a thirty-three-year-old father of five whose livelihood depends on his ability to track down and club to death at least fifteen mature tuna in the coming twenty-four hours. Tooth-brushing came late to the Maldives, but the practice has taken hold as firmly as the executives of Colgate-Palmolive could have hoped, thanks in part to a television campaign featuring a shark with vividly gleaming dentition.

The tube lives on a shelf in the fishing boat's combined kitchenette-toilet. At breakfast time, we join the crew in the main cabin for a freshly cooked meal, our first in many days. *miruhulee boava* (octopus tentacles) followed by an invitation to chew a bunch of areca palm leaves.

After breakfast comes a succession of
card games. The tuna below us have a few
more hours in which to partake of life
on the planet. It should not be presumed
from this image that the author is in any
way lacking in empathy or bonhomie, or
that he would be unable (as is sometimes
suspected of intellectuals) to take his
place, man to man, amongst a group of
illiterate Indian Ocean sailors exchanging
anecdotes in an unfathomable Indo-
Sanskrit tongue. He is merely in that
preoccupied state, of necessity involving
a distant gaze and extreme concentration,
which often accompanies attempts to
control runaway intestinal inflammation.

For hours we wander the sea without hope. Then shortly after eleven in the morning – dawn in the warehouse in the middle of England – a school of yellowfin tuna approach from the east, swimming in a V-shape, the older, more confident fish on the outside, the younger ones inside. They are moving at fifty kilometres an hour, on their way to Somalia from the coasts of Indonesia. Because they lack a swim-bladder, the cursed creatures have no option but to advance relentlessly; they cannot pause and rest on the current, like the sedate grouper, or they would fall to the bottom of the ocean and die, only growing more attractive to man by their continual exertions, for it is through the life-long flexing of their tails that their flesh grows muscular and hence uniquely flavoursome. A cry goes up on deck. One of the school, by all indications a heavier, older specimen, a veteran of five years of unmolested navigation, has taken a bite at a bait of mackerel. Fifteen minutes later, he announces himself on the starboard side, panicked and enraged, his tail hammering against the boat. Fifty kilos in weight, he is attempting to prise himself free of the cable tearing apart his palate, but he does not count on two men, above him at either end, reaching into the water with steel hooks and flipping him onto the deck with a victorious cry. Pandemonium follows.

The tuna has never been this far out of the water, has never seen light this bright, but he knows instinctively that he will drown in so much air. The fishermen need him to stop flooding his arteries with blood in panic, or he will darken, and therefore ruin, the appearance of his flesh against a dinner plate. So the captain's brother swiftly wrestles him between his rubber boots and raises aloft a large, blunt mallet, resembling the archetypal club of a prehistoric man, carved from the trunk of a coconut tree. He brings it down heavily. The tuna's eyes jerk out of their sockets. His tail convulses. His jaw opens and closes, as ours might do, but no scream emerges. The mallet strikes again.

There is a dull sound, that of densely packed brain and experience, shattering inside a tight bony cage, triggering the thought that we too are never more than one hard slam away from a definitive end to our carefully arranged ideas and copious involvement with ourselves. The fisherman is himself enraged now, striking the beast vengefully, cursing the dying creature in Dhivehi: '*Nagoobalha, nagoobalha, hey aruvaalaanañ*' ('Bitch, bitch, you've had it now'). This is the first tuna he has caught in eight days, and there are six children waiting at home.

Rich red blood explodes from the creature's brain and sprays across the boat. Two of the younger crewmen rush forward and slit open his mouth, pulling out his gills and ventilation system. Next they turn their knives to his stomach, releasing the undigested bodies of smaller fish – fusiliers, cardinal fish, sprats – on which he breakfasted at the start of this infernal day. The deck becomes slippery with organs. As the killing spree goes on, I find myself thinking obsessively of my elder son, four years old and about the same length as some of the larger fish. It is no longer implausible that, as many religions maintain, we are all in the end, from moth to president,

members of the same large, irrevocably fratricidal family. Unburdened of his guts and his reproductive tract, the tuna is hoisted into the air and plunged into the first of four refrigerated compartments, which will, by nightfall, be filled by the bodies of a further twenty of his companions. One wonders what the atmosphere will be like in the school, 60 metres below, as the survivors pursue their way to Somalia; whether there will be a memory of the absent members and, in the pitch-black waters, a terrible fear.

We arrive at the fish processing plant – which keeps in close touch with British importers and supermarkets. The true nature of bureaucracy may be nowhere more obvious to the observer than in a developing country, for only there will it still be made manifest by the full complement of documents, files, veneered desks and cabinets – which convey the strict and inverse relationship between productivity and paperwork. Despite cautionary tales from a range of antecedents from Gauguin to Edward Said, I am unable wholly to suppress fleeting images of a joint future with Salma Mahir, the secretary of the owner of the plant, who harbours as many misconceptions about my country as I do about hers. My Maldivian father looks on.

The boss of the tuna plant, when he finally arrives, is an unexpected phenomenon. In temperament, Yasir Waheed combines the phlegmatic romanticism of a late-nineteenth-century French poet with the carnivorous aggression of a contemporary Anglo-American capitalist. His favourite book, by Bill Zanker and Donald Trump, is *Think Big and Kick Ass in Business and Life*. He is just back from an electronics conference in Dubai, where he picked up a Bluetooth wireless mouse for his Apple Cinema.

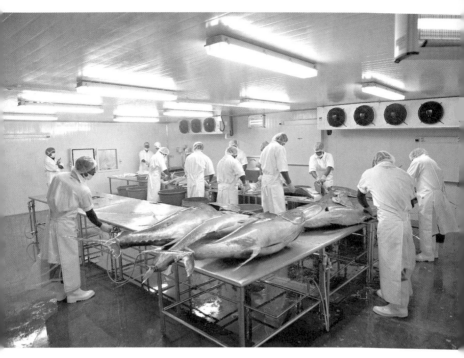

The plant's fish handlers know how to fillet a tuna with machetes in three minutes. All were once fishermen. The sound of one of their knives cutting flesh away from a spine recalls that of a fingernail strumming the teeth of a comb. All are now widowers. Yasir took pity on them after seeing them weeping on the news after the tsunami rolled round the eastern shores of Sri Lanka and swept away their families when they were out at sea. While there are clear medical and hygienic reasons, in the preparation of fish for export, for requiring that plant workers' facial hair be covered by surgical masks, that the temperature be kept constantly below zero degrees centigrade and that all aprons and other work garments be incinerated after a single wearing, it may nevertheless be a reflection of something more deeply embedded in the Western soul that it is we who have ended up as the unparalleled masters of artificial chilling techniques, of continual hand-washing and of rampant hygienic imaginations.

Like someone running into an old friend
in a strange land, I am surprised and a
little moved when I stumble across a reel
of bright-orange labels long familiar to
me from my local supermarket. With
the picture of the fishermen clubbing
tuna to death burnt into my memory,
I recognise that I am now a veteran
of the blood-soaked processes lurking
behind the labels' serene photograph
of a fishing jetty and an azure sea.

There being only so many efficient ways
to cut through air or water, the architecture of the plane evokes aspects of the
tuna. The Airbus has gill-like air-inlet
flaps near its wheels and fins along its
fuselage. Even the lower bodies of the
two creatures are a comparable piscine
grey. One crate is locked in place below
rows 3 and 9 in business class, the other
below rows 43 and 48 in economy. On
the apron beside the London-bound
Sri Lankan jet is a Qatar Airways cargo
plane, its windows painted out, on its
way around the world, bearing post,
vegetables, documents and blood samples.

The plane was in Tokyo last night and
is due in Milan Malpensa tomorrow,
one of thousands of freighters which,
without any acknowledgement on our
arrival and departure screens, pursue
their lonely routes around the earth.

We take off at 8:30 a.m. and head north-west across the Indian Ocean. Outside, to the untrained and unaided eye, the plane appears to be adrift above an unsubstantial, vaporous blue mass, as featureless and disorienting as the sea but, reconfigured through the antennae of the flight-deck instruments (comparable in their abilities to the organic mechanisms embedded in the tuna's cranium at the spot where the fisherman's mallet fell), the sky is revealed as a lattice of well-marked lanes, intersections, lay-bys, junctions and beacon signals. The plane races along airway A418, which runs from the Gulf into southern Iran.

Over the town of Shiraz, in a space known to pilots as intersection SYZ117.8, the captain moves across to airway R659, which leads to UMH113.5, a point thirty-five thousand feet above Uromiyeh, the capital of western Azerbaijan, where the Three Wise Men are said to have rested on their way to Bethlehem.

The cabin crew serve red chicken curry in Economy and a choice of asparagus vol-au-vent or cheese omelette in Business. The skies darken. Occasionally, one catches sight of the very moment when a light is extinguished in a house below. Someone has finished watching television in a living room in Craivoa, Romania, someone in Kalocsa, Hungary, has reached the end of an article in the fashion magazine *Nok Lapja*, neither of them suspecting the existence of an aluminium missile roaring through the firmament above them.

I look at others' faces and feel sympathy towards them. People stir under their synthetic blankets. If we lived still in the days of ocean liners, we might all be friends by the time we docked at Southampton.

The plane lands at Heathrow at nightfall. The tuna makes it to the warehouse by two in the morning, revealing nothing to a succession of men in high visibility jackets about its tumultuous history of aquatic and airborne wandering. The drivers in the warehouse never know at the start of a shift where they may find themselves by dawn. At four in the morning, Ian Cook receives a command from the control room to drive one of the largest of the articulated lorries over to Bristol. The driver has been doing supermarket runs for the last fifteen years. He carries his belongings in a small red bag and has a complicated life, for he has a wife in Lancashire and a friend in Derby. He talks continually on the journey, covering murderers, religious zealots, tax evaders and child molesters, in a monologue whose unarticulated yet nonetheless powerful guiding theme is the decline and eventual collapse of contemporary civilisation. By early morning, the lorry comes to a stop at the back of an aluminium shed in suburban Bristol, on whose aisles the tuna is placed, fifty-two hours after it was first levered out of the aphotic brine of the Indian Ocean.

The photographer and I crouch in wait behind a refrigerated cabinet, which feels vengefully cold after the torridity of the Maldives. Shoppers amble by, occasionally casting a distracted look at the cuts of the tuna's flesh. To pass the time, I think back to people we have met along the way. I remember Aisha Azdah, whose job it is to source the tuna's packaging material. She ordered the plastic trays from a manufacturer in Thailand. One afternoon, we photographed her in her one-room company flat next to the processing plant. On the wall is her wedding picture, featuring Mohamed Amir, a mechanic in charge of the tuna slicing machines made by the Scanvaegt corporation of Denmark. The interest of the photograph seems to hinge on the iron. This is an essay about people who depend on one another and yet have no thought of each other's laundry. It may be one of the tasks of art in the age of advanced logistics to make sure that Aisha is introduced to Linda Drummond, for in the end, it is she who stops at the fish counter and picks up some tuna steaks for her family's supper. The photographer and I stand up and explain our story. We tell her about our journey and about Karl Marx's theory of alienation as defined his *Economic and Philosophic Manuscripts of 1844*. We ask if we might follow her home. She calls her husband for a second opinion.

Later that day, Linda's son, eight-year-old Sam, is unfazed to find two strangers in his kitchen. He hates tuna, but not as much as he hates salmon. He hasn't forgotten about the wonder of logistics. He knows a lot about lorries and planes. He is also an expert on the world's oceans, and lectures us as to how the Indian Ocean is not an ideal habitat for fish, on account of its unusual warmth and stillness. He notes that the freezing North Sea supports infinitely more forms of life, as storms there constantly stir up the nutrient-laden aphotic layer which lies a thousand metres below the waves, and in which the gulper eel, the anglerfish and the vampire squid live.

He also makes the ancillary suggestion, less often remarked upon by marine biologists, that our perpetual killing of fish has left the seas choked with an array of pallid oceanic ghosts who will one day gather together to exact terrible revenge on humanity for shortening their lives and transporting their corpses around the earth for supper in Bristol.

III

Biscuit Manufacture

1.

I became interested in biscuits and one day found myself heading out to the west of London, past burnt-out shops and roped-off demolition sites, to the town of Hayes, the corporate home of United Biscuits, the number-one player in the British biscuit market and its second-largest producer of bagged nuts.

Through effort and subterfuge, I had secured an appointment with the Design Director at United Biscuits, a man named Laurence (rather than Lawrence, a distinction he repeatedly emphasised). To prepare for my encounter, I had immersed myself in the distinctive literature of biscuits and learnt a range of intriguing facts. I had discovered that the British spend £1.8 billion a year on biscuits, and that the market is technically divided into five categories: Everyday Biscuits, Everyday Treats, Seasonal Biscuits, Savoury Biscuits and Crackers & Crispbreads.

Everyday Biscuits, despite their lacklustre name, account for nearly a third of all sales and include Digestives, Rich Tea, Ginger Nuts and Hob Nobs. The Digestive, often dipped in tea for added moisture, is alone worth £34 million a year. For their part, Everyday Treats, evenly poised between the ordinary and the indulgent, are typically bought on Thursdays and Fridays by women between thirty-five and forty-four and number among their rank Jaffa Cakes, Cadbury's Fingers and Fox's Chocolate Viennese. As for Seasonal Biscuits, they are marketed only between the start of October and the end of December and come in highly decorated tins that comprise combinations of Cottage Crunch, Shortcake, Shortbread Finger and Chocolate Chip biscuits.

Much to the frustration of experts in both fields, Crackers & Crispbreads and Savoury Biscuits are routinely confused. To be clear, Crackers & Crispbreads are non-sweet biscuits intended to be eaten either as part of a diet or as an accompaniment to cheese or a spread, while Savoury Biscuits are to be enjoyed on their own and offer greater interest than standard crackers, usually thanks to the addition of a cheese or barbecue flavour. Activity in this final category has tended in recent years to be focused on the introduction of diminutive products such as the Mini Cream Cheese and Chive, the Baked Mini Cheddar and the Snack-A-Jack Mini Barbecue.

2.

Hayes itself was surprisingly devoid of charm. There were few restaurants, only one bowling alley and no cinemas. Such were the limitations of the place, a young woman I met in the course of my research told me that she would only ever accept a date with someone in nearby Hillingdon – a town which did not for that matter, at least on a cursory drive through it, strike me as having any notable advantages over its neighbour.

The biscuit company occupied a three-storey beige-brick building on a business park. It had for the previous five years been owned by a pair of private equity firms, one of which, the Blackstone Group, was headed by a financier legendary for buying the most expensive duplex in the history of Manhattan. Among the company's most popular brands were McVitie's, go ahead!, Twiglets, Hula Hoops, McCoy's and KP Nuts. It also produced the prawn-flavoured cocktail snack Skips, known for its uniquely fizzy reaction with human saliva. A brochure in the lobby explained that United Biscuits took its social responsibilities seriously and that it had, through its Jaffa Cake Division, donated a number of shirts with logos on them to an under-seven football team in the town of Ruislip.

Laurence met me by the lifts, under the shadow of a giant bag of crisps. He was a volatile mixture of confidence and vulnerability. He

could deliver extended monologues on professional matters, then promptly stop in his tracks to peer inquisitively into his guest's eyes for signs of boredom or mockery, being intelligent enough to be unable fully to believe in his own claims to significance. He might, in a past life, have been a particularly canny and sharp-tongued royal advisor. One might have supposed that our mutual premature baldness would have led to a rapprochement, but the shared disability only generated an unwanted point of identification.

Laurence led me to the boardroom where a table had been scattered with boxes of Moments, a six-centimetre-wide biscuit made of chocolate and shortcake, launched in the spring of 2006 at a ceremony (during which Laurence had made a speech in French) in a manufacturing plant in Belgium, following a two-year-long, £3 million development programme. Laurence was the biscuit's author.

3.

This was not to say that Laurence knew how to bake, though he grew swiftly defensive in response to my expression of surprise at his inability. Biscuits are nowadays a branch of psychology, not cooking, he advised sternly.

Laurence had formulated his biscuit by gathering some interviewees in a hotel in Slough and, over a week, questioning them about their lives, in an attempt to tease out of them certain emotional longings that could subsequently be elaborated into the organising principles behind a new product. In a conference room in the Thames Riviera hotel, a number of low-income mothers had spoken of their yearning for sympathy, affection and what Laurence termed simply, with aphoristic brevity, 'me-time'. The Moment set out to suggest itself as the plausible solution to their predicament.

While the idea of answering psychological yearnings with dough might seem daunting, Laurence explained that in the hands of an experienced branding expert, decisions about width, shape, coating, packaging and name can furnish a biscuit with a personality as subtly and appropriately nuanced as that of a protagonist in a great novel.

Early on, it became evident to Laurence that his biscuit would need to be round rather than square, given the associations drawn in almost all cultures between the circle and feminity and wholeness. It was similarly imperative that it contain small pieces of raisin and whole chocolate chips to convey an impression of kindly indulgence – though because it was not outright decadence which was being evoked, no cream would be involved.

Laurence spent a further half a year working with colleagues on dilemmas of packaging, eventually resolving that a mere nine biscuits should be settled into a black plastic tray encased in a glossy twenty-four-centimetre-long cardboard box. Laurence now initiated a debate about what to call the biscuits. Extensive consideration was given to Reflections, Retreats, Delights and, in a direct allusion to the biscuit's founding concept, My Times – before the right name came to Laurence in what could kindly be described as a flash of inspiration.

It was time for attention to be paid to the choice of fonts. The designers' initial layout had had the word Moments running in a romantic Edwardian script across the box, but there were concerns among some executives that this belied the product's projected function as a pleasant supplement to real life rather than a means of escape from it – an issue addressed by a last-minute change in the *m* and *s* to a more vertical orientation, as befitted a snack which respected the realities of life even as it offered temporary relief from them.

4.

It is perhaps because many of us know what it is to spend an afternoon baking biscuits that there is something striking about encountering a company which relies on the labour of five thousand full-time employees to execute the task.

Manoeuvres which one might briefly have carried out on one's own in the kitchen (readying an oven, mixing dough, writing a label) had at United Biscuits been isolated, codified and expanded to occupy entire working lives. Although all employment at the company was ultimately predicated on the sale of confectionery and salted snacks, a high percentage of the staff were, professionally speaking, many times removed from contact with anything one might eat. They were managing the forklift truck fleet in the warehouse or poring over the eighty or so words written along the sides of a typical packet of salted nuts. Some had attained extraordinary expertise in the collection and analysis of sales data from supermarkets, while others daily investigated how to ensure a minimum of friction between wafers during transit.

Along with such specialisation came a raft of esoteric job titles: Packaging Technologist, Branding Executive, Learning Centre Manager, Strategic Projects Evaluator. Careers ploughed along deep and dedicated furrows: a start at Hula Hoops might be followed by promotion to Ridged Tortillas, a sideways shift to Baked Mini Cheddars, a management role at McVitie's Fruitsters and a swan-song post at Ginger Nuts.

The unremitting division of labour resulted in admirable levels of productivity. The company's success appeared to bear out the principles of efficiency laid down at the turn of the twentieth century by the Italian economist Vilfredo Pareto, who theorised that a society would grow wealthy to the extent that its members forfeited general

knowledge in favour of fostering individual ability in narrowly con-
stricted fields. In an ideal Paretan economy, jobs would be ever more
finely subdivided to allow for the accumulation of complex skills,
which would then be traded among workers. It would be in everyone's best interest that doctors not waste time learning how to fix
boilers, that train drivers not sew clothes for their children and that
Biscuit Packaging Technologists leave questions of warehousing to
graduates in supply-chain management, the better to concentrate
their own energies on the improvement of roll-wrap mechanisms.
In a perfect society, so specialised would all jobs be, that no one
would any longer understand what anyone else was doing.

During a series of often bewildering conversations with members
of staff, I came to realise that a Paretan utopia was now a realistic
prospect at United Biscuits. But however great the economic advantages of segmenting the elements of an afternoon's work into a range
of forty-year-long careers, there was reason to wonder about the
unintended side effects of doing so. In particular, one felt tempted
to ask – especially on sombre days when the eastward-bound clouds
hung low over the head office in Hayes – how meaningful the lives
might feel as a result.

5.
When does a job feel meaningful? Whenever it allows us to generate
delight or reduce suffering in others. Though we are often taught
to think of ourselves as inherently selfish, the longing to act meaningfully in our work seems just as stubborn a part of our make-up
as our appetite for status or money. It is because we are meaning-
focused animals rather than simply materialistic ones that we can
reasonably contemplate surrendering security for a career helping
to bring drinking water to rural Malawi or might quit a job in con-

sumer goods for one in cardiac nursing, aware that when it comes to improving the human condition a well-controlled defibrillator has the edge over even the finest biscuit.

But we should be wary of restricting the idea of meaningful work too tightly, of focusing only on the doctors, the nuns of Kolkata or the Old Masters. There can be less exalted ways to contribute to the furtherance of the collective good and it seems that making a perfectly formed stripey chocolate circle which helps to fill an impatient stomach in the long morning hours between nine o'clock and noon may deserve its own secure, if microscopic, place in the pantheon of innovations designed to alleviate the burdens of existence.

The real issue is not whether baking biscuits is meaningful, but the extent to which the activity can seem to be so after it has been continuously stretched and subdivided across five thousand lives and half a dozen different manufacturing sites. An endeavour endowed with meaning may appear meaningful only when it proceeds briskly in the hands of a restricted number of actors and therefore where particular workers can make an imaginative connection between what they have done with their working days and their impact upon others.

It is surely significant that the adults who feature in children's books are rarely, if ever, Regional Sales Managers or Building Services Engineers. They are shopkeepers, builders, cooks or farmers – people whose labour can easily be linked to the visible betterment of human life. As creatures innately aware of balance and proportion, we cannot help but sense that something is awry in a job title like 'Brand Supervision Coordinator, Sweet Biscuits' and that whatever the logic and perspicacity of Vilfredo Pareto's arguments, another principle to which no one has yet given a convincing name has here been ignored and subtler human laws violated.

6.

Matters were compounded because, whatever the modesty of the ends at United Biscuits, the means to produce the Moments and their siblings nevertheless required the dedication and self-discipline that might otherwise have been called upon to run a hospital or become a ballerina. A question of motivation appeared: whether the company could succeed in providing its staff with a sufficiently elevated set of ideals in whose name they were to exhaust themselves and surrender the greatest share of their lives.

Many of the proceedings at United Biscuits had to them an air of gravity akin to that which might obtain in an airport control tower. This was because, for all their questionable taste and negligible nutritional value, biscuits made money – and in the sort of quantities which would have overwhelmed the exchequers of the greatest monarchs of history. To look at the biscuit profit figures in the light of graphs by the modern historian of the Tudors, Sir Geoffrey Elton, the company was pulling in more money in profits *every year* than Henry VIII and Elizabeth I had succeeded in doing in their entire reigns combined – all this from a beige-brick office block in the north-eastern corner of Hayes, only twenty minutes by car from the gilded state rooms of Hampton Court.

Accordingly, even the head of the Blackstone private equity group (a man whose personal fortune outstripped the wealth of all the kingdoms of sub-Saharan Africa since the discovery of fire), had on occasion left behind his penthouse in order to genuflect before pastry. The company headquarters might have borrowed its aesthetic from a roadside motel, but only because, unlike the inhabitants of Versailles and the Escorial palace (distracted as they had been by thoughts of God, power and beauty), the leaders of the biscuit company harboured no doubt as to which divinity they were worshipping.

Perhaps for this reason, I was to encounter no jokes at any biscuit's expense. The minders of the Ginger Nut and the Rich Tea, of the Jaffa Cake and the Moment, resembled a flock of patient, grave-faced courtiers ministering to the needs of a nursery of wilful infant emperors.

7.

Late one afternoon, after darkness had fallen across the business park in Hayes, rendering particularly visible the lights of aircraft (many of them wide-bodied jets coming in from Asia) as they descended towards Heathrow, I passed by a corner office in which an employee was typing up a document relating to the brand performance of the Moments range. It had been almost a year since the biscuit's launch. Renae's expression was thoughtful and absorbed, and though I could not immediately have said why, something about her brought to mind a painting by Edward Hopper which I had seen several years before at the Museum of Modern Art in Manhattan.

In *New York Movie* (1939), an usherette stands by the stairwell of an ornate pre-war theatre. Whereas the audience is sunk in semidarkness, she is bathed in a rich pool of yellow light. As often in Hopper's work, her expression suggests that her thoughts have carried her elsewhere. She is beautiful and young, with carefully curled blond hair, and there are a touching fragility and an anxiety about her which elicit both care and desire. Despite her lowly job, she is the painting's guardian of integrity and intelligence, the Cinderella of the cinema. Hopper seems to be delivering a subtle commentary on, and indictment of, the medium itself, implying that a technological invention associated with communal excitement has paradoxically succeeded in curtailing our concern for others. The painting's power hangs on the juxtaposition of two ideas: first, that the woman is more interesting than the film, and second, that she is being ignored *because* of the film. In their haste to take their seats, the members of the audience have omitted to notice that they have in their midst a heroine more sympathetic and compelling than any character Hollywood could offer up. It is left to the painter, working in a quieter, more observant idiom, to rescue what the film has encouraged its viewers not to see.

A comparable dynamic seemed in play in the head office at Hayes, where there was a marked imbalance between the importance accorded to the supposed centres of interest – the biscuits – and the neglected value of humans like Renae who laboured to meet their demands. I wondered whether the biscuits might not be part of the very problem that they had been designed to address, whether their production and marketing was not indeed contributing to precisely the feelings of emptiness and nervous tension which they claimed to alleviate.

I wondered out loud to Renae why in our society the greatest sums of money so often tended to accrue from the sale of the least meaningful things, and why the dramatic improvements in efficiency and productivity at the heart of the Industrial Revolution so seldom extended beyond the provision of commonplace material goods like shampoo or condoms, oven-gloves or lingerie. I told Renae that our robots and engines were delivering the lion's share of their benefits at the base of our pyramid of needs, that we were evident experts at swiftly assembling confectionery and yet we were still searching for reliable means of generating emotional stability or marital harmony. Renae had little to add to this analysis. A terrified expression spread across her features and she asked if I might excuse her.

Later, caught in a traffic jam on my way out of Hayes, in a landscape of discount-furniture warehouses and chemical storage tanks,

I lost my temper and wished a biblical plague on the house of biscuits, so that its directors might learn to tremble before the right
gods. I remembered a passage from John Ruskin's *The Crown of Wild
Olive,* written in 1866, eighty-one years before the invention of the
Jaffa Cake: 'Of all wastes, the greatest waste that you can commit
is the waste of labour. If you went down in the morning into your
dairy, and you found that your youngest child and the cat were at
play together, and that the boy had poured out all the cream on the
floor for the cat to lap up, you would scold the child, and be sorry
the milk was wasted. But if, instead of wooden bowls with milk in
them, there are golden bowls with human life in them, and instead
of leaving that golden bowl to be broken by God at the fountain, you
break it in the dust yourself, and pour the human blood out on the
ground for the fiend to lick up – that is no waste! What! you perhaps
think, "to waste the labour of men is not to kill them." Is it not? I
should like to know how you could kill them more utterly'.

Well-meaning friends advised me that I appeared to be slipping
into an unfamiliar and somewhat hysterical mood, and might benefit
from an interval of less stressful 'me-time'.

8.

A week later, I received notice that the senior management of
United Biscuits had approved my request to visit the factory where
the Moments were manufactured, at a site in eastern Belgium, in
hilly farming country between Verviers and the German border.

I chose to spend a few days driving there and so took a ferry
to Ostend, then meandered along minor roads, stopping off at the
occasional zoo or heraldic museum, afraid that I might otherwise
leave Belgium sooner than I had planned. However, when it came
to meals, I ran scared of the forced intimacy that provincial family

restaurants so often involve and chose instead to eat in the ano-
nymity of motorway service stations. At one of these, on the E40,
I met a Turk who was driving a consignment of dates from Izmir
to Copenhagen. We started chatting after I parked my car next to
his articulated lorry, beside which he was shaving with a high-end
Braun machine that cast a haunting green light across his face.
Because I admired his chrome-plated cherry-coloured juggernaut,
he invited me to have a look inside its cab, which had a small bunk-
room at the rear fitted out with brightly coloured kilims, carved
teak panelling and a window that looked out onto an incongru-
ously flat northern European landscape on which a herd of Friesian
cows was grazing.

In Liège, I booked in to the Holiday Inn, a concrete block which
hovered on the outskirts of the town, seemingly fearful of entering its medieval centre and keenly nostalgic for the architecture of
Detroit or Atlanta. In the evening, I ordered a breaded chicken esca-
lope from room service, and ate it whilst sitting on my bed, reading
a book on the history of art in the Low Countries. Some time past
midnight, I began watching a television programme made up of a
rolling succession of illustrated personal ads submitted by members
of the public, including a baker from Charleroi who was on the look
out for 'l'amour et un peu plus', a programme which continued for
several hours deep into an insomniac night and revealed levels of
longing that I had not until then suspected from my brief exchanges
in this small and fractured nation.

The next morning, I woke up, still tired, to the sounds of a
vacuum cleaner outside. Dressed in a towel, I opened the door and
saw a trolley and an abandoned room-service tray on which sat the
strangely appetising remnants of a hamburger and fries. The door
opposite was ajar and I glimpsed two cleaners inside laughing ani-

matedly while they worked. Seeing them strip the bed, I remembered the book I had read the previous night, which had detailed the way in which the seventeenth-century artists of the region had sought to celebrate the skills involved in domestic service, honouring in particular the scrubbing of kitchens and courtyards, privileging such activities over more conventionally prestigious biblical subjects.

By the time I was ready to go down to breakfast, the neighbouring room had been transformed. It had been turned into an immaculate history-less space awaiting its next occupant, motionless except for particles of dust whirling on the back of invisible eddies of air in a shaft of morning sunlight.

As often happens before an important appointment, I arrived far too early at the biscuit factory in the village of Lambermont – and so drove to a nearby archaeological museum, where I learnt about flint and axe manufacture in Neolithic Belgium. There were records of nasty disagreements and, in one display cabinet, the remains of a man whose head had been broken open with an axe, and who had been found by archaeologists curled up in a defensive position, hugging himself from the blows of his opponent. The agony of death long ago became so vivid that the importance and solidity of the present were for a time thrown into doubt.

Because my appointment to tour the factory had been scheduled to start at the ambiguous hour of twelve-thirty, I had earlier that morning given thought to whether I might be offered lunch or should eat beforehand, eventually deciding to make some cheese sandwiches at the breakfast buffet, a snack I now ate in the car while listening to a radio interview with the Belgian finance minister.

When I pulled up at the gates of the plant, Michel Pottier, the manager, was waiting for me in person, carrying with him a spare white gown, a pair of rubber shoes and a hairnet, an outfit forced

upon all visitors which, by giving one a sense of adhering to an extreme millenarian movement, was apt to lend a peculiar tone to conversations.

A warm-hearted and garrulous figure, Pottier had prepared a second lunch for me in a corner of his office, and expected a hearty appetite, so I consumed three additional sandwiches and several Moments which had come off the line only that morning. As we ate, Pottier took me through some of the challenges attendant on the making of biscuits, placing special emphasis on the need to cool the dough rapidly enough to prevent it from melting the chocolate with which it would subsequently be coated. Years of working around noisy machinery had left my host mildly deaf in one ear and given him a concomitant habit of leaning in uncomfortably close during discussions, so close that I began to dread his enunciation of a word with a *p* or a *g* in it. Pottier's disquisitions on topics such as the plant's annual biscuit tonnage and the ideal viscosity of chocolate did not always accurately gauge the levels of interest of his interlocutor, but they communicated clearly enough a surprisingly intense pride in the plant and its workers.

Alongside the Moment, the factory also supplied a number of leading brands for the European market, including Delichoc, Gateau and Teatime. Pottier informed me that this last, a chocolate-covered digit, had recently been marketed in a limited-edition tin bearing an image of two minor members of the Belgian royal family cradling their newborn baby.

When we entered the main production hall, I was reminded of the peculiar feeling I had experienced in other factories upon seeing modestly sized domestic objects emerge from the jaws of colossal machines housed in hangars large enough for airships. Biscuits which I had until then seen only in packets of nine were here rolling down the conveyor belt at a rate of eleven hundred a minute. A polydimensional sprinkler was enrobing the Moments in chocolate whilst another porcupined them with small shards of nuts. The technology behind this machinery had been borrowed from applications as disparate as the machine gun, the stapler, the space shuttle's robotic arm and the loom. A mixer was kneading six thousand tonnes of dough as an adjacent contraption assembled thirty-five thousand brightly coloured biscuit cartons per hour.

This mechanisation had been introduced not so much because human beings were unable to perform the tasks in hand, but because labour had grown prohibitively expensive. Economics dictated the superior logic of hiring a few engineers to develop three-armed hydraulic machines, then firing two-thirds of the staff and paying them unemployment benefits so that they could stay at home watching television, subsidised by revenues from corporation taxes paid by the likes of United Biscuits.

One felt in the presence of so much that consumers who slit open their packets of Moments would be unlikely to imagine. For example, the windowless hall, filled with a gentle aroma of sugar and chocolate, where two middle-aged women in hairnets sat facing each other over a moving rubber carpet, looking out for the smallest fault in the texture of dough, and occasionally reaching over to pick out an offending biscuit, their concentrated stares suggesting that they were engaged in a tense game of drafts. Their work nevertheless left them with enough energy for conversation: one was telling the other that her son was, in spite of his family's advice to the contrary, still going out with a slut obsessed by clothes and the tanning salon (she didn't sound uninteresting), as serried ranks of biscuits passed by, to unsung fates in boardrooms in Dundee or nursing homes in Poole.

Then there was Hassan, whose job it was to keep watch on a mixer as high as a house, adding vegetable fat to flour as necessary, and who had arrived in Belgium from a village in western Algeria three months before. There was also the forlorn bus stop outside the factory, from where workers departed to neighbouring villages and towns, and the remarkable presence of nature all around the factory, with a horse in an adjoining field gazing lazily up to the corporate flag of United Biscuits, which flapped like a flannel in an icy breeze.

The factory was an economic entity, no doubt, but it was also a product of architecture, psychology and ethnography. One wondered whether its owners at the Blackstone Group were aware of the full implications of owning a tract of the earth and the largest share of the lives of two hundred people in eastern Belgium, and whether an imaginative recognition of these facts ever crossed their minds when they glanced at the profit-and-loss figures in their offices in Manhattan and whether they might even, at the close of their careers, derive a particular pleasure and a sense of responsibility from their investment unconnected to any financial considerations.

Most of Pottier's efforts focused on keeping the factory line rolling at all times. The previous summer, when temperatures had reached forty degrees centigrade indoors, he had had to borrow a row of air-conditioning units from the Belgian air force to protect his chocolate. Stray hairs were a constant concern and necessitated weekly lectures to staff on the correct use of their cotton hats. Nevertheless, there had been three expensive interruptions to the line in the run-up to Christmas, caused by false alarms when black hair-like bristles fixed to the ends of certain machines had come loose, incidents which had prompted Pottier to install a set of new brushes, finished in a vivid orange colour seldom seen on the human head.

The care and skill which Pottier brought to his occupation reinforced the point made in the book I had been reading the previous evening, with its analysis of two contrasting approaches to work found in the histories of Protestant and Catholic thought. In Catholic dogma, the definition of noble work had mostly been limited to that done by priests in the service of God, with practical and commercial labour relegated to an entirely base category unconnected to the display of any specifically Christian virtues. By contrast, the Protestant worldview as it had developed over the sixteenth century attempted to redeem the value of everyday tasks, proposing that many apparently unimportant activities could in fact enable those who undertook them to convey the qualities of their souls. In this schema, humility, wisdom, respect and kindness could be practised in a shop no less sincerely than in a monastery. Salvation could be worked out at the level of ordinary existence, not only in the grand, sacramental moments which Catholicism had privileged. Sweeping the yard and arranging the laundry cupboard were intimately related to the most significant themes of existence.

Pottier animated the Protestant ideal. His manner drew attention away from what he was doing in favour of how he was doing it. His approach suggested that there might be a continuity, rather than an insurmountable barrier, between work at the top and bottom of the ladder of meaning – and that many of the talents exercised in the most exalted tasks were no less likely to be found inside a steel hangar reverberating with the sound of dough-mixers and chocolate-coating machines.

9.

Partially undermining the manufacturer's ability to assert that its work constituted a meaningful contribution to mankind was the frivolous way in which it went about marketing its products. Grief was the only rational response to the news that an employee had spent three months devising a supermarket promotion based on an offer of free stickers of cartoon characters called the Fimbles. Why had the grown-ups so churlishly abdicated their responsibilities? Were there not more important ambitions to be met before Death showed himself on the horizon in his hooded black cloak, his scythe slung over his shoulder?

Yet before ridiculing the Branding Director of Savoury Biscuits, or for that matter the Special Events Manager who had signed off on the tinned assortment featuring Prince Philippe and Princess Mathilde of Belgium on its lid, it was wise to remember that at the heart of biscuit salesmanship lay an imperative which was undoubtedly both urgent and simple enough to qualify as meaningful – namely, survival. Workers were occupied with the ancient task of trying to stay alive, which simply happened to require, in a consumer economy overwhelmingly based on the satisfaction of peripheral desires, a series of activities all too easily confused with clownishness.

Despite a few years of healthy profits, United Biscuits' balance sheet was perennially vulnerable. Following the closures of all local steel, textile and coal industries, the area around the factory had some of the worst unemployment figures in the European Union, and accompanyingly high rates of crime and suicide. Any miscalculation in branding or manufacturing techniques, or a sudden increase in the price of wheat, or an irregularity in the supply of cocoa, could at a stroke wipe out a section of the workforce, who

would be unlikely ever to find adequate labour locally again. Pottier knew what responsibility he shouldered for his people. He expressed particular concern at the predatory behaviour of his main competitor, the misleadingly cosy-sounding LU brand, owned by the gigantic French Danone Group. The two enterprises regularly locked horns like stags fighting to the death over a limited habitat, in this case, the ten or so metres of the typical biscuit-aisle in the supermarkets of Northern Europe. Their respective sales teams waged sly campaigns to steal each other's market share. Every product which United Biscuits made in Belgium was imitated by LU: its Delichoc, a butter biscuit coated in chocolate, faced off against LU's Le Petit Écolier; its plain butter biscuit Gateau went head to head with LU's Le Petit Beurre; and its chocolate-and-orange Colombine was countered by LU's Pim's Orange, even as its Domino, a wafer cookie with a chocolate cream filling, contended for its existence with LU's Le Fondant.

The manufacture and promotion of all of these was no game, but rather an attempt to subsist which was no less grave, and therefore no less worthy of respect and dignity, than a boar hunt on whose successful conclusion the fate of an entire primitive community might once have hung. For if a new wrapping machine did not operate as efficiently as anticipated, or if a slogan failed to capture the imagination of shoppers, there would be no escape from shuttered houses and despair in the suburbs of nearby Verviers. The biscuits carried lives on their backs.

Modern commercial endeavours may not be of the kind that we have been taught to associate with heroism. They involve battles fought with the most bathetic of instruments, with two-for-the-price-of-one specials and sticker-based bribes, but they are battles nonetheless, comparable in their intensity and demands to the tracking of furtive animals through the deadly forests of prehistoric Belgium.

10.

I travelled back to England along the route used weekly by a fleet of articulated lorries transporting shipments of Moments from their plant to the United Biscuits distribution centre at Ashby de la Zouch. Near Ostend, I stopped off at a service station whose forecourt was lined with trucks heading for the cross-Channel ferries.

I lapsed into thoughts of factories across the continent involved in making breadsticks and candles, rubber bands and butter, lasagne and batteries, pillow cases and toy boats – and in turn, I imagined trucks that would at that moment be crossing Europe, travelling north with fondue sets, west with hi-fi parts, underneath the Alps with cellophane and around the Bay of Biscay with puff cereal.

At the end of a field opposite the service station ran the high-speed Thalys rail line, on which bullet trains sped at 250 kilometres an hour between the Netherlands and France, each machine costing some 28 million euros. Inside, passengers might have been reading papers and having a drink (maybe a Pepsi Light, a Tropicana Mixed Fruit Vitalité, a Fanta Lemon or a Schweppes Dry Orange), while outside, the shadows of trees flickered in the dusk like the projected images of early films. What a peculiar civilisation this was: inordinately rich, yet inclined to accrue its wealth through the sale of some astonishingly small and only distantly meaningful things, a civilisation torn and unable sensibly to adjudicate between the worthwhile ends to which money might be put and the often morally trivial and destructive mechanisms of its generation.

It was in the eighteenth century that economists and political theorists first became aware of the paradoxes and triumphs of commercial societies, which place trade, luxury and private fortunes at their centre whilst paying only lip-service to the pursuit of higher goals. From the beginning, observers of these societies have been

transfixed by two of their most prominent features: their wealth and their spiritual decadence. Venice in her heyday was one such society, Holland another, eighteenth-century Britain a third. Most of the world now follows their example.

Their self-indulgence has consistently appalled a share of their most high-minded and morally ambitious members, who have railed against consumerism and instead honoured beauty and nature, art and fellowship. But the premises of a biscuit company are a fruitful place to recall that there has always been an insurmountable problem facing those countries that ignore the efficient production of chocolate biscuits and sternly dissuade their ablest citizens from spending their lives on the development of innovative marketing promotions: they have been poor, so poor as to be unable to guarantee political stability or take care of their most vulnerable citizens, whom they have lost to famines and epidemics. It is the high-minded countries that have let their members starve, whereas the self-centred and the childish ones have, off the back of their doughnuts and six thousand varieties of ice cream, had the resources to invest in maternity wards and cranial scanning machines.

Amsterdam was founded on the sale of raisins and flowers. The palaces of Venice were assembled from the profits of the carpet and spice trades. Sugar built Bristol. And yet despite their frequently amoral policies, their neglect of ideals and their selfish liberalism, commercial societies have been graced with well-laden shops and treasuries swollen enough to provide for the construction of temples and foundling hospitals.

At my window seat in the motorway service station outside Ostend, observing the departure of a lorry carrying toilet rolls to Denmark, I opened a box of Moments that Pottier had presented to me as a farewell gift and thought about societies where exceptional fortunes are built up in industries with very little connection to our sincere and significant needs, industries where it is difficult to escape from the disparity between a seriousness of means and a triviality of ends, and where we are hence prone to fall into crises of meaning at our computer terminals and our warehouses, contemplating with low-level despair the banality of our labour while at the same time honouring the material fecundity that flows from it – knowing that what may look like a childish game is in fact never far from a struggle for our very survival. All of these ideas seemed embedded in an unexpectedly comforting set of glutinous, chocolate-coated Moments.

IV

Career Counselling

1.

However powerful our technology and complex our corporations, the most remarkable feature of the modern working world may in the end be internal, consisting in an aspect of our mentalities: in the widely held belief that our work should make us happy. All societies have had work at their centre; ours is the first to suggest that it could be something much more than a punishment or a penance. Ours is the first to imply that we should seek to work even in the absence of a financial imperative. Our choice of occupation is held to define our identity to the extent that the most insistent question we ask of new acquaintances is not where they come from or who their parents were but what they *do*, the assumption being that the route to a meaningful existence must invariably pass through the gate of remunerative employment.

It was not always this way. In the fourth century BC, Aristotle defined an attitude that was to last more than two millennia when he referred to a structural incompatibility between satisfaction and a paid position. For the Greek philosopher, financial need placed one on a par with slaves and animals. The labour of the hands, as much as of the mercantile sides of the mind, would lead to psychological deformation. Only a private income and a life of leisure could afford citizens adequate opportunity to enjoy the higher pleasures gifted by music and philosophy.

Early Christianity appended to Aristotle's notion the still darker doctrine that the miseries of work were an appropriate and immovable means of expiating the sins of Adam. It was not until the Renaissance that new notes began to be heard. In the biographies of great artists, men like Leonardo and Michelangelo, we hear the first references to the glories of practical activity. While this re-evaluation was at first limited to artistic work and even then, only to its most exalted examples, it came in time to encompass almost all occupations. By the middle of the eighteenth century, in a direct challenge to the Aristotelian position, Diderot and d'Alembert published their twenty-seven-volume *Encyclopédie*, filled with articles celebrating the particular genius and joy involved in baking bread, planting asparagus, operating a windmill, forging an anchor, printing a book and running a silver mine. Accompanying the text were illustrations of the tools employed to complete such tasks: among them pulleys, tongs and clamps, instruments whose precise purpose readers might not always understand, but which they could nonetheless recognise as furthering the pursuit of skilful and dignified ends. After spending a month in a needle-making workshop in Normandy, the writer Alexandre Deleyre produced perhaps the most influential article in the *Encyclopédie*, in which he respectfully described the fifteen steps required to transform a lump of metal into one of those deft and often overlooked instruments used to sew on buttons.

Purported to be a sober compendium of knowledge, the *Encyclopédie* was in truth a paean to the nobility of labour. Diderot laid bare his motives in an entry on 'Art', lambasting those who were inclined to venerate only the 'liberal' arts (Aristotle's music and philosophy) whilst ignoring their 'mechanical' equivalents (such as clock-making and silk-weaving): 'The liberal arts have sung their own praise long enough; they should now raise their voice in praise of the mechanical arts. The liberal arts must free the mechanical arts from the degradation in which these have so long been held by prejudice.'

The bourgeois thinkers of the eighteenth century thus turned Aristotle's formula on its head: satisfactions which the Greek philosopher had identified with leisure were now transposed to the sphere of work, while tasks lacking in any financial reward were drained

Here, too, possibilities for happiness:
'Forging an anchor', from Diderot and D'Alembert's *Encyclopédie*

of all significance and left to the haphazard attentions of decadent dilettantes. It now seemed as impossible that one could be happy and unproductive as it had once seemed unlikely that one could work and be human.

Aspects of this evolution in attitudes towards work had intriguing parallels in ideas about love. In this sphere too, the eighteenth-century bourgeoisie yoked together what was pleasurable and what was necessary. They argued that there was no inherent conflict between sexual passion and the practical demands of raising children in a family unit, and that there could hence be romance within a marriage – just as there could be enjoyment within a paid job.

Initiating developments of which we are still the heirs, the European bourgeoisie took the momentous steps of co-opting on behalf of both marriage and work the pleasures hitherto pessimistically – or perhaps realistically – confined, by aristocrats, to the subsidiary realms of the love affair and the hobby.

2.

It was with this history in mind that I became interested in meeting a career counsellor, a professional dedicated to finding ways of ensuring that work will be synonymous with fulfilment.

An internet search produced a company called Career Counselling International, whose website promised help for those facing 'troubling life decisions and occupational choices'. This authoritative claim led me to expect large and well-appointed headquarters, but the company turned out to be run from the back of an unassuming and cramped Victorian home in a run-down residential street in South London. It featured a small administrative office and a consulting room with Paul Klee prints and views of a clotted carp pond and a washing line. The only full-time employee, Robert Symons, a fifty-five-year-old psychotherapist, had started the business twelve years before, and ran it along with his wife, June, who helped with the accounts and the marking of aptitude tests. The couple were admirably fond of some of the less popular vegetables in the English repertoire, for at most times of the day – even in the early morning – the place smelt powerfully of freshly boiled cabbage or swede. Symons had studied psychology at Bristol University, where he had come under the influence of the humanistic school of psychology which emphasised creativity and self-development. In his spare time, he had written a book entitled *The Real Me: Career as an Act of Selfhood*, which he had been trying to publish for several years.

Symons was a tall and bearded man who looked as if he could wrestle a wolf to the ground, but his physical might belied the patient manner of a priest. In another era, one imagined him as the curate of a peaceful rural parish, keeping bees and a tortoise in the garden, believing in little, but ministering with exceptional sincerity to the needs of the sick and the troubled. In the consulting room, we sat facing each other across a plate of fig rolls, for which he confessed an almost addictive fondness. So kindly were his eyes, he seemed like someone who would be open to confessions of the most unusual sort. Not even the most extreme quirk of the mind appeared liable to surprise him or elicit humiliating judgement. I harboured a confused wish for him to be my father.

Three days a week, Symons saw private clients in his house and, on the remaining two, he visited businesses around the country, advising workers about to be laid off or managers who were having difficulty shouldering their responsibilities. He also offered motivational seminars for the unemployed, psychometric testing for interviews and, from a stand at university careers fairs, sessions with graduates preparing to enter the job market.

We agreed that I should observe his working methods over a number of weeks. I would accompany him on his travels and, via a video monitor in the administrative office (with the necessary permissions in hand), observe his consultations with his clients. All he asked in return was that I should recommend him the name of an effective literary agent.

3.

Three days later, I was ensconced in a tight cupboard that served for a study, looking at a black-and-white screen showing the events unfolding in the consulting room next door, where the first client of the day had begun summing up her personal history and professional dissatisfactions with a compelling mixture of formality and honesty. There were papers and files stacked up to the ceiling all around me and, on the floor, a bag of Symons's sports equipment, emitting the strong smell of recently used gym shoes. The client's voice could be heard both through the loudspeaker on the monitor and more directly through the walls. It was one of those crystalline, perfectly enunciated English voices, the sort one might acquire growing up in Walton-upon-Thames and graduating with a First in History from Keble College, Oxford. Through a slit in the door, I could see the client's coat hanging in the hall, a rich blue cashmere garment freckled with water, along with a slim leather briefcase.

Three times the client interrupted her own anecdotes, suddenly pushing back her hair and saying, 'I'm so sorry, this must be unbearably boring', to which Symons shot back calmly, as if he had been expecting her to say this all along, 'I am here only for you'. Twenty minutes into the session, the therapist dropped his voice almost to a whisper and asked, with an avuncular warmth, what had become of the spontaneous and excited child the client must once have been.

At which, quite without warning, Carol, thirty-seven years old, a tax lawyer, in charge of a department of forty-five in an office near the Bank of England, began to sob, as Symons watched her with his kindly eyes and, outside, the neighbour's cat took a stroll around the carp pond.

After Carol had left, as Symons threw away a pile of used tissues and rearranged the cushions on the couch, he remarked that the most common and unhelpful illusion plaguing those who came to see him was the idea that they ought somehow, in the normal course of events, to have intuited – long before they had finished their degrees, started families, bought houses and risen to the top of law firms – what they should properly be doing with their lives. They were tormented by a residual notion of having through some error or stupidity on their part missed out on their true 'calling'.

This curious and unfortunate term had first come into circulation in a Christian context during the medieval period, in reference to people's abrupt encounter with an imperative to devote themselves to Jesus' teachings. But Symons maintained that a secularised version of this notion had survived even into the modern age, where it was prone to torture us with an expectation that the meaning of our lives might at some point be revealed to us in a ready-made and decisive form, which would in turn render us permanently immune to feelings of confusion, envy and regret.

Symons preferred a quote from *Motivation and Personality*, by the psychologist Abraham Maslow, which he had pinned up above the toilet: 'It isn't normal to know what we want. It is a rare and difficult psychological achievement.'

4.

When Carol returned the following week, she was dressed in a green skirt and t-shirt and seemed a decade younger. Symons apologised for the smell in the room (his wife was making puréed swede with cheesy crust) and suggested that she submit to a small written exercise. He put in front of her three sheets of blank paper headed 'Things that I Like', and gave her ten minutes to make a list of everything which came into her head, from the grand to the seemingly inconsequential, while he went off to get them some lemon-and-ginger tea, having always resisted the Freudian injunction against overfamiliarity between therapist and client.

Carol filled in her sheets, often breaking off to look out of the window. She had the strong, almost masculine beauty one might have associated with the wife of a middle-ranking colonial administrator in Uganda in the 1920s.

Symons knew that it was hopeless to try to guide people towards more fulfilling vocations simply by discussing with them directly what they might like to do. Concerns about money and status would long ago have extinguished most clients' ability to think authentically about their options. He preferred for them to return to first principles and free-associate around clusters of concerns that delighted and excited them, without attempting to settle upon them anything as rigid as the frame of a career.

Symons had a metaphor he favoured: in searching for their aptitudes, his clients were to act like treasure hunters passing over the ground with metal detectors, listening out for what he called beeps of joy. A man might get his first intimation that his real interest lay in poetry not by hearing the command of a holy voice as he paged through a book of verse, but from a beep he experienced at the sight of mist over a quiet valley seen from the top of an edge-of-town carpark. Or a politician, long before she belonged to any party or had any profound understanding of statecraft, might register a telling signal when successfully healing a rift between two members of her family.

As it happened, Carol's beeps turned out to be perplexingly varied. Her reveries about what she liked included visiting old churches, giving presents, making things neat, eating in a fish restaurant set up by a friend in Margate, buying old chairs and reading blogs about economics on the internet.

Carol and Symons devoted several sessions to interpreting the list, bringing to the task some of the detachment of a pair of archaeologists assigned to study the rubble of an ancient town. The more they talked about the fish restaurant, the clearer it became that it wasn't the place, in itself, that held any special appeal for Carol; what impressed her was the example of someone who had taken the risk to build a business around a personal interest. Symons took from this exchange the word *passion,* which he penned on a whiteboard affixed to the back of the door. As for Carol's love of economics blogs, this was with time revealed to be anchored around an enthusiasm for just one particular example dealing with issues of social entrepreneurship. Symons wrote *altruism and business* on the board.

Counsellor and client now turned their focus to envy. Symons was a particular admirer of this feeling, and lamented the way that its useful role in alerting us to our possibilities was too often censored out of priggish moralism. Without envy, there could be no recognition of one's desires. So Symons gave Carol another ten-minute slot to list everyone she most regularly envied – adding on his way out of the room that he didn't care for niceness and that if there were not at least two names of close colleagues or friends

on her piece of paper, he would know that she had been evasively
sentimental.

Watching these sessions on closed circuit television, I came to
feel that what was unfolding in the damp room next door was of his-
torical significance. Symons had devoted his life to paying an exceptional degree of attention to the most minor feelings of another
person. After millennia in which action had been privileged over
reflection, and intelligence primarily restricted to the discussion of
arid abstract ideas, an ordinary human's everyday confusions had at
last found a forum in which they were being accorded the methodi-
cal consideration they deserved. Among all the other, better-estab-
lished businesses catering to elements far down our hierarchy of
needs – businesses offering assistance with gardening and cleaning, accountancy and computers – here, finally, was an enterprise
devoted to the interpretation of the critical, yet troublingly indistinct, radio-transmissions of the psyche.

Above Symons's desk was a photograph of Michelangelo's
unfinished sculpture entitled *'Atlas' Slave*, from the collection of the
Accademia Gallery in Florence. In this block of stone, arrested
midway on its journey from raw material to museum piece, an as-
yet-headless human figure is seen struggling to emerge from a chunk
of marble. The partially completed object appealed to Symons as a
metaphor for what he believed that career counselling might do for
all of us: in Nietzsche's words, help us to *become* who we *are*.

5.

A month into my time with him, Symons asked if I might like to
follow him on a working trip to the north of England. Our first stop
would be Newcastle, where he had reserved a space at a university's careers fair. Two thousand students were expected to wander

through a Victorian hall filled with employers from every sector of the economy and Symons would be offering half-hour consultations, with the option of subsequent discussions over the telephone.

The train from London was packed, so the ticket collector – taking pity on us as we stood in the corridor with large bags holding the components of Symons's booth – let us into the first-class compartment, where we sat in deep velour-covered armchairs and were served a breakfast of sausages and eggs. Far from cheering Symons up, however, the unanticipated luxury seemed to bring out a melancholic side in him which I had not previously seen. As the remains of industrial England passed by outside the window, he brooded over the debased state of modern culture and manners. Then, shifting his focus, he spoke of how few people were willing to invest in his services, and how few of those engaged him for more than a single introductory session or opted for anything other than his test-based methods of counselling, on the basis of their cost and speed. Most Britons were resigned to spending their entire adult lives working at jobs chosen for them by their unthinking sixteen-year-old selves, he concluded, while across the aisle, in apparent confirmation of this analysis, a teenage girl languidly leafed through the celebrity pages of *Bella* magazine.

We reached the careers fair just as the doors were being opened, and hurried to assemble our stand. Students streamed in, often in high spirits, travelling in gangs and regularly erupting with threatening guffaws. Their obvious good health and, in some cases, beauty served to suggest that knowledge and experience might not, in the end, be very valuable commodities to take refuge in.

A few passers-by picked up leaflets as they brushed past the stand, but most moved on in a hurry, headed for a defence contractor and a supermarket chain across the way. An unprofitable and

wearing day seemed to be confirmed when, in the late afternoon, Symons went through a pile of introductory questionnaires that he had handed out only to discover that one of them had been filled in by Søren Kierkegaard. In the box headed 'What I would like to achieve in my career', the nascent comic had written, 'To overturn the hegemony of pseudo-Christian values and the hypocrisy of the established Danish Church'.

We retreated that evening to a joyless Ibis hotel where the dining room had closed due to a flood and, after a cheese sandwich from a petrol station, turned in early.

Matters began to look up the next day, however, when we went to Middlesbrough to visit a windscreen repair company which was in the process of laying off twenty-five middle managers. The bosses had asked Symons to conduct a seminar entitled 'Self-Confidence', during which he would lead the redundant workers through a number of exercises designed to help them to imagine an adequate future for themselves. In the morning session, he projected some slides onto a screen: *I can do anything if I put my mind to it. I can be strong and move mountains. I can set myself goals and achieve them. Nothing I have done so far is an indication of the powers that are within me.* These were supplemented by a booklet Symons handed out, containing extracts from the biographies of famous self-made men and women. On the fly-leaf was a quote from Leon Battista Alberti: *A man can do all things if he will.*

None of this was easy to watch, and several times I found myself looking awkwardly out of the window at the cafeteria below. I was particularly troubled to hear one participant repeating, under Symons's direction: *I am the author of my own story.* In the bathroom to which I repaired for mental relief, I tried to analyse my discomfort, and yet in so doing, began to be suspicious of my own stance.

I realised that Symons's talk unsettled me because it reflected a disturbing but ultimately unavoidable truth about achievement in the modern world. In older, more hierarchical societies, an individual's fate had largely been decided by the accidents of birth; the difference between success and failure had not hung on a proficiency with the declaration *I can move mountains.*

However, in the meritocratic, socially mobile modern world, one's status might now well be determined by one's confidence, imagination and ability to convince others of one's due – a possibility of advancement which shone a less flattering light on philosophies of stoicism and resignation. It seemed that one might squander one's life chances because of a high-handed disdain for books with titles such as *The Will to Succeed*, believing that one was above their shrill slogans of encouragement. One might be doomed not by a lack of talent, but by a species of pessimistic pride.

After lunch, Symons took his managers back into the lecture room and offered them a chance to share their hopes for the future, the idea being that a public revelation of this kind would stand as a promise to themselves which would be the harder to break when their confidence wavered. An employee in her early forties, who had been with the company for twenty years, spoke of her ambition to open a tea shop in the village where she had grown up. So strong was her enthusiasm, and so detailed were her plans (the walls were to be hung with pictures of the young Shirley Temple), that it was almost impossible not to feel stirred. I *can* move mountains, she concluded by saying, and returned to her seat, to the applause of all the participants.

I felt my eyes fill. I was reminded that whatever over-cerebral understanding we may sometimes apply to our functioning, we nevertheless retain some humblingly simple needs, among them a prodigious and steady hunger for support and love. It was to the archaic part of our personalities that Symons's motivational exercises appealed, the side which requires neither eloquence nor complex logic and which will forgive ungainly sentences so long as they are imbued with the necessary, redemptive doses of hope.

Towards the end of the day, Symons engaged his audience in a discussion about what he called the voices of despair, internalised attitudes emphasising the chances of failure. Many of the participants traced such voices back to an unhelpful parent or a disapproving teacher, someone who, decades before, had subjected them to criticism or neglect. One after another, grown men and women rose to their feet to recount how, when they were barely the height of a door handle, they had suffered some grievous injury to their self-image: a maths teacher had berated them for their poor algebra skills, or a father had said that it was their sister who was good at art and that they should stick to sport instead.

The evidence suggested that the forming of an individual in its early years was as sensitive and important a task as the correct casting of a skyscraper's foundations and that the slightest impurity introduced at a primary stage could possess a tyrannical power to unbalance a human animal until its dying days. To continue to deny the significance of barely perceptible childhood abuses was to manifest the same robust and foolhardy common-sense which had once led our ancestors to scoff at the notion that there might be deadly colonies of microorganisms thriving in drops of saliva no larger than pinheads.

Seen from this perspective, the weight accorded to ideas of nurture and to the development of self-esteem in theories of modern education no longer seemed like a sign that our societies had gone mad or soft. On the contrary, this emphasis was as finely attuned to the demands of contemporary working life as instruction in stoicism and physical bravery had been to the exigencies of ancient times.

It owed its existence less to kindness than to practical necessity. Like the rearing methods of every age, it was intended to ensure that the young would be granted the optimal chances of survival in a hostile environment.

6.

A few weeks after we returned from the north, I travelled with Symons to an office in central London, where he had been commissioned by an American bank to put some job applicants through a morning's worth of tests. Symons had hoped that this process could be combined with a more informative round of face-to-face interviews, but the bank turned out not to want to expend the requisite time and resources. The tests would be scored overnight and a decision taken on hiring the following day.

Symons's subjects devoted the bulk of their session to filling out the Morrisby Personality Profile, the most respected and widely used of all aptitude questionnaires. Never far from doubting the wisdom of my own career choice, I joined the candidates in the hope of learning more about my working psyche. I searched for exceptions within lists of words and tried to solve visual puzzles and analogies such as '*Heavy* is to *light* as *a) wide b) day c) jump* is to *d) brick e) narrow f) house*'.

Which wheel turns the fastest when the tractor moves?

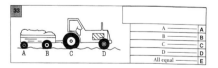

Which of these identical ships have the heaviest load?

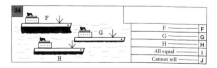

Two days later, my test results came back from Symons's office in an exclusively bound folder designed to assert the importance of their conclusions. Held up against the subtlety of the psychological exchanges I had observed between Symons and Carol (who had since handed in her resignation from her law firm and applied for a managerial post with a housing charity), the report felt like it had been written by a computer. 'The candidate displays average abilities which would render him well-suited to a range of middle-ranking administrative and commercial posts', the document began, before it singled out a particular talent for marketing and a weakness with numbers. 'His future may lie in one of the following fields: medical diagnostics, oil and gas exploration or the leisure industry'.

I recognised my desire to submit to the report's conclusions in the hope of quelling my doubts about my future. At the same time, the report failed to inspire any real degree of confidence and indeed, the more I dwelt on it, the more it seemed to signal some of the limits of career counselling as a whole. I thought again about the smells of cabbage and swede in Symons's office. It struck me as strange and regrettable that in our society something as prospectively life altering as the determination of a person's vocation had for the most part been abandoned to marginalised therapists practising their trade from garden extensions. What should have been one of the most admired professions on earth was struggling to attain the status open to a travel agent.

But perhaps this neglect was only an appropriate reflection of how little therapists can in the end make sense of human nature. An understandable hunger for answers from potential clients tempts many of them to overpromise, like creative writing teachers who, out of greed or sentimentality, sometimes imply that all of their students could one day produce worthwhile literature, rather than frankly acknowledging the troubling truth, so anathema to a democratic society, that the great writer, like the contented worker, remains an erratic and anomalous event, no less immune to the methods of factory farming than a truffle.

The true range of obstacles in the way of unlocking our potential was more accurately acknowledged by the German sociologist Max Weber when, in his essay 'Science as a Vocation' (1918), he described Goethe as an example of the sort of creative and healthy personality 'who appears only once in a thousand years'.

For the rest of history, for most of us, our bright promise will always fall short of being actualised; it will never earn us bountiful sums of money or beget exemplary objects or organisations. It will remain no more than a hope carried over from childhood, or a dream entertained as we drive along the motorway and feel our plans hovering above a wide horizon. Extraordinary resilience, intelligence and good fortune are needed to redraw the map of our reality, while on either side of the summits of greatness are arrayed the endless foothills populated by the tortured celibates of achievement.

Most of us stand poised at the edge of brilliance, haunted by the knowledge of our proximity, yet still demonstrably on the wrong side of the line, our dealings with reality undermined by a range of minor yet critical psychological flaws (a little too much optimism, an unprocessed rebelliousness, a fatal impatience or sentimentality). We are like an exquisite high-speed aircraft which for lack of a tiny part is left stranded beside the runway, rendered slower than a tractor or a bicycle.

I left Symons's company newly aware of the unthinking cruelty discreetly coiled within the magnanimous bourgeois assurance that everyone can discover happiness through work and love. It isn't that these two entities are invariably incapable of delivering fulfilment, only that they almost never do so. And when an exception is misrepresented as a rule, our individual misfortunes, instead of seeming to us quasi-inevitable aspects of life, will weigh down on us like particular curses. In denying the natural place reserved for longing and error in the human lot, the bourgeois ideology denies us the possibility of collective consolation for our fractious marriages and our unexploited ambitions, and condemns us instead to solitary feelings of shame and persecution for having stubbornly failed to become who we are.

7.

In the end, twelve literary agents read Symons's manuscript. All replied politely and with encouragement. *The Real Me: Career as an Act of Selfhood* remains without a publisher.

V

Rocket Science

1.

In August 2007, on a humid tropical afternoon, an Air France jet touched down in French Guiana, carrying in its Business-class cabin twelve senior executives from a Japanese television company, who had flown from Tokyo to South America to follow the launch of their satellite.

The executives had bought the machine to help them start a new kind of television station, which they hoped would seize the imagination of the Japanese public and overturn the dominance of the state broadcaster NHK, legendary for its narrow focus on lengthy films about the cherry blossom season and the hunting habits of the Tibetan tiger. They had in mind a station that would show *anime* films about the exploits of warrior robots and romantic dramas about precociously seductive school-girls. They wanted game-shows that would mete out sadistic punishment to their losers and soap operas that would blow open the lid on the extramarital longings of the wives of salarymen living along Tokyo's commuter lines.

But Japanese topography has traditionally created insurmountable challenges for anyone seeking entry into the broadcasting market, for the country is dispersed across four main islands, most of which are heavily forested and prone to storms and volcanic eruptions, conditions requiring investment in prohibitively expensive maintenance facilities – which helps to explain why, for most of the post-war period, Japanese television has remained unchallenged in the hands of the staid, cherry-blossom-loving, government-owned behemoth.

However, the pioneering executives imagined a way around the logistical hurdles. They discovered that if they fired a satellite into space and, in particular, induced it to settle into an orbit at 110 degrees east, thirty-six thousand kilometres above the ground, they would then be able to beam down a signal to anyone with a modestly priced dish anywhere across their archipelago. A show such as *Sensei No Kaban*, about the illicit love affair between a twenty-year-old woman and her seventy-five-year-old calligraphy teacher, could be transmitted into the upper atmosphere and bounced back to reach both the icy mountains of Hokkaido and the palm and skyscraper-fringed coastline of Okinawa.

And so evolved the idea for Japan's first satellite television station, a business whose very name was intended – as the channel's mission statement put it – to inspire in its viewers 'an expression of constant wonder and amazement': WOWOW TV. But there would be a host of further tribulations in translating the business plan into a reality, including struggles with government officials and regulators, painful equity deals with the Nippon Corporation and Fuji Incorporated, and fraught negotiations to secure broadcast rights to the popular Korean TV drama *My Name Is Kim Sam Soon*. Finally, there was a protracted search for an actual satellite, which, after pitches from rival companies and a process not much more dignified than a haggle in a souk, led to the purchase, from the Lockheed Martin Corporation, of a $100 million A2100A model, a device now awaiting its first meeting with its new owners in a hangar in a jungle clearing a few kilometres away from the airport.

2.

The Japanese television executives filed off the plane, past a photograph of the French President and into a VIP zone where they were greeted, with all the respect and warmth due to anyone who has lately handed over a launch fee close to $75 million, by bowing senior members of the French commercial space agency Ariane Espace. After clearing customs and formerly entering French

Guiana, the executives were each handed a large wooden box containing a silver replica of their satellite and led out to a minibus bound for their hotel.

It was evident that they had arrived in a peculiar corner of the world. The difficulties with French Guiana begin with trying to place it on a map. Seldom has a country been as easily and as regularly confused with somewhere else: Ghana on the western coast of Africa, Guyana east of Venezuela, Guinea next to Senegal, the former Portuguese colony of Guiné next to Guinea now referred to as Guinea-Bissau, Equatorial Guinea below Cameroon or the island of New Guinea divided between Indonesia and Papua New Guinea. Even the pronunciation is prone to engender trouble, the English referring to the country as French Guiana (Guy-arna) while the French favour a more compacted Guyane (Gü-yann).

More significantly, the territory bears the surreal burden of being at once located on the malarial northern coast of South America, between Surinam to the west and Brazil to the south, whilst also belonging to the French state, having been absorbed into one of the country's twenty-six *départements* by its former colonial master in 1946. As a result, it is now a member of the European Union, its highest legal authority is the Court of Justice in Strasbourg, its agricultural and fishery policies are defined in Brussels and its currency, valid even in the Indian settlement of Pilakoupoupiaina on the Oyapock River, is the euro, from the European Central Bank of Frankfurt-am-Main.

A layer of French bureaucracy and bourgeois ambition has been unevenly applied across this tropical kaleidoscope. In tin-roofed villages, *terrains de boules* abut voodoo temples. The country's only two roads, Routes Nationales 1 and 2, are fitted out with standard French signs, whose font, Frutiger 57 Condensed, is more accus-

tomed to pointing the way to Nantes or Clermont-Ferrand but here twists itself around Amerindian place-names such as Iracoubo and Awala-Yalimapo. Restaurants (Café de la Gare, Bar Chez Pierrot) serve escalopes of wild jungle boar and Amazonian river fish with the scaly appearance of prehistoric coelacanths, cut into fillets and domesticated under a *meunière* sauce.

Deprivation and despair is everywhere apparent. The country has no economy to speak of. There is neither tourism, for the sea is plagued by sharks and brown from river sediment, nor, thanks to the poor quality of the soil, any agriculture. The roads down to Brazil are largely impassible and the territory's sole reliable outlet to the world is the daily flight to Paris (a trip to nearby Venezuela or Peru requiring a connection in Orly).

3.
Proud of their achievements and generous of spirit, the WOWOW television executives had given permission for a small group of us to follow them on their journey.

A Hong Kong television station sent one of its most prominent young reporters accompanied – due to budgetary pressures – by only a one-person crew, who bore the contents of a studio on his back, leaving the elegant presenter (something of a household name in her city), to wander around in silver high-heeled shoes, her face frozen in a distressed expression, perhaps not unlike that worn by Amiral Estrées, the earliest French colonist of French Guiana, at the moment when he realised that the country was not to be the El Dorado which Sir Walter Ralegh had led him to expect from his conspicuously mistitled book, *The Discoverie of the Large, Rich and Bewtiful Empire of Guiana,* first published in London in 1595.

Ten rocket engineers from NASA had flown down from Florida as part of an exchange programme. Burdened by a sense of their own spatial superiority, they felt a pervasive need not to humiliate their hosts by any allusions to their agency's achievements or the scale of its resources and so bore the unfailingly courteous and humble manner reminiscent of royalty on a tour of a slum district. They engaged in elaborate praise of their counterparts' most routine achievements, like their ability to build a petrol station or to install air conditioning – though the patronisation seemed to whistle blithely past the French, who were in their hearts no less firmly, if a little less shyly, convinced of their own greatness.

We had all been billeted together in the Atlantis Hotel which, though only newly built, was fast surrendering itself to tropical mould and the incursions of jungle fauna. Vivid yellow lizards scuttled across the hotel's floors and on returning to the room late at night, it was not uncommon to be confronted by a muscular and implausibly furry spider standing stationary on the wall above the television, a situation resolved by a Creole maintenance man who dispatched the monster with a decisive slap of rolled-up newspaper, leaving nothing but a brown sediment to commemorate the presence, then tossed the corpse off the balcony and, with apparent sincerity, bade one a pleasant end to the evening.

Kourou, the purpose-built town next to the space centre, was in no better shape than the hotel on its perimeter. Evoking comparison with Chandigarh and Brasilia, two other examples of modern architecture's impressive track record of indifference to issues of context and culture, it was in an advanced stage of decomposition after only a few decades of existence. Unshaded wooden benches rotted unused by the man-made lake, having been designed to provide respite on the kind of afternoon stroll which it had not yet occurred

to anyone in the tropics to take, whilst the concrete façades of buildings had buckled in a climate which from April to July could deliver in a single week as much rainfall as northern France might see in an entire year.

4.

However, once inside the heavily fortified gates of the space centre itself, the situation was transformed. Immaculate buildings were dedicated to the assembly of satellites, the preparation of Ariane boosters and the storage of propellants. These were scattered across hectares of marsh and jungle, generating bewildering contrasts for visitors who might walk out of a rocket-nozzle-actuator building and a moment later find themselves in a section of rain forest sheltering round-eared bats and white-eyed parakeets, before arriving at a propulsion facility whose corridors were lined with Evian dispensers.

Early on our first morning in the country, we were driven to a hangar not much smaller than Reims cathedral where we caught our first glimpse of the satellite, resting on a central platform, bathed in a powerful white light, being ministered to by a congregation of engineers in gowns, hairnets and slippers. They were filling the satellite's tanks, charging its batteries and testing its transponders. Given the cost of carrying matter into space, it was surprisingly modest in size, a box measuring just four metres high by two wide, flanked by a pair of fourteen-metre long solar panels topped by a reflecting dish. Its inner works consisted of an electric motor, some thrusters to help counteract the effects of solar wind and twelve 130-watt broadcast channels with which to beam down an electronic footprint of WOWOW TV's programming.

To be allowed into the satellite's presence, we were requested to undertake purification rituals akin to those required for admittance to an operating theatre, for the machine was a curious synthesis of robustness and hypersensitivity. At the speed it would soon be travelling – 3.07 kilometres per second – a stray human hair inside one of its transponders could create a disastrous force field of electromagnetic energy or a single oily fingerprint could fissure its solar panels. The satellite was like a frontline soldier who could be reduced to tears by reading a children's book, though in fairness, its vulnerability obtained only under the eccentric conditions of outer space, where powerful ultraviolet rays and clusters of oxygen atoms were capable of exploiting any weakness in an electrical system, and where extreme variations in temperature, from 200 degrees centigrade in the sun to minus 200 in the earth's shadow, could crack any part of the machine which had not been immaculately cleaned and wrapped in a protective carapace of gold-tinted polyimide film.

Raised up on its dais – its surfaces seeming to emit a pinky-red glow, its compartments opened to reveal dense wiring, the whole assembled out of such unfamiliar components as pyromellitic acid – the satellite looked like one of the most unnatural objects imaginable. Yet in truth it contained nothing which had not been present on the earth in the earliest days of creation, nor anything which had not (in its basic form, at least) originally been lodged in the chemical structures of the seas and mountains. It was the cogitations of the human mind which had cooked and recombined the planet's raw materials into this most unlikely offering to the heavens.

5.

The sight of different groups of hairnetted engineers helping to prepare the satellite suggested what restraint, what effacement of

the individual ego, a life in science now entailed. There were no opportunities for individual glory here, no prospect of biographies or street names to be remembered by. This was a collective project for which no one person, not even any single commercial or academic organisation, could take the commanding credit.

Gone were the days of geniuses in their observatories and workshops, single-handedly rerouting scientific history. We had entered the sober era of the collaborative laboratory, where astrophysicists and aeronautical engineers banded themselves together for decade-long assaults on minor mysteries, resisting the media's attempts to raise any one of their number into a contemporary Galileo. A company might limit itself to perfecting the performance of silver-zinc batteries in zero-gravity conditions, rightly sensing the foolishness of expanding to address further puzzles in satellite electrics. A scientist might spend a lifetime examining the properties of titanium at high temperatures or the behaviour of hydrogen at the moment of ignition. The sum total of one's contributions to mankind might end up in an issue of the *Journal of Advanced Propulsion Methods*.

Some of the technical properties of WOWOW TV's new machine were the result of research done in the early 1980s by a team of scientists from Milan Polytechnic, who, in investigating the use of the upper reaches of the electromagnetic spectrum in communications satellites, had found a way around the interference caused by low cloud and misty rain at microwave frequencies above 10 gigahertz – slow and unheroic work that now, a quarter of a century later, ensured that Japanese viewers would be able to enjoy the uncut version of the *anime* film *Cowboy Bebop* even during the worst downpours in Japan's rainy season.

Though there had certainly been a loss of colour and novelistic detail in the passing of the age of geniuses, there was perhaps something greater and more reassuring in our graduation to a time of collective effort, for it meant that never again would the fate of planetary exploration depend to a hazardous degree on such unpredictable variables as the mood of Johannes Kepler's wife Barbara or the inclinations of his patron Emperor Rudolf II — though the German astronomer, like many of his fellow geniuses, had at least provided Kourou with a name for one of its dispiriting streets, a rectangle of waste ground bordered by a dry cleaner at one end and a burnt-out internet café at the other, a matter in which the collated proponents of later discoveries would perhaps never be quite so obliging.

6.

Just a short drive away through the jungle, two thirty-metre-high booster rockets were undergoing their penultimate preparations. These delicately tapered structures, decorated with the flags of the European nations which had contributed to their funding, would be responsible for propelling the satellite on the first stage of its journey. They were in truth more bombs than engines, for they had no throttle and once ignited, had to be allowed to expend their full fury, whatever the circumstances, inspiring a particular respect in all those involved in their detonation.

Dr Thierry Proudhon was directing operations. He held a degree in pyrotechnics from the National School of Aeronautical Engineering in Toulouse and had been living in French Guiana with his family for three years. A finely chiselled man in his early forties, he seemed about as reasonable, impersonal and solemn as it is possible for any human to be, given the follies and convulsions to which our race appears prone. Not for him the torments of the insomniac or the agitations of the neurotic. On the day of the launch, he would be responsible for the ignition of 500 tonnes of ammonium

perchlorate composite, which would burn for only 130 seconds, but would in that time succeed in firing the fifty-two-metre-high Ariane launcher 150 kilometres into the sky, generating a thrust of 1,100 tonnes and a concomitant boom which would be heard over the border in Brazil. Then, their titanic energies spent, the boosters would detach themselves from the mother ship and drop down into the Atlantic ocean, where a French naval frigate would be standing by to collect them.

Prompted by a question from the Hong Kong television presenter, but chary of the sensationalist tenor of her enquiry, Dr Proudhon paused for a moment to consider what might 'go wrong', responding with all the austerity of a chemistry teacher reviewing the risks of the Bunsen burner before an assembly of excitable pupils. He explained that if the propellant paste were incorrectly mixed in such a way that it retained air pockets, it could produce a sudden increase in the surface area of flammable material and a corresponding rise in exhaust gases, which might well have the power to rupture the casing of the rocket and cause an explosion equivalent in its short-term destructive force to that of a small nuclear device. But, he added to reassure – and thereby also, inadvertently, to disappoint – his audience, there was only a 0.2 percent chance of such an incident's occurring on any given launch.

At a loss as to how to return to the salient topic, but unwilling to conclude the conversation, the presenter asked what this mysterious propellent substance might look like. Was it a little like toothpaste? Or perhaps more like cake mix? Dr Proudhon fixed her with his grey-green eyes and, answering the query at the level of detail he felt the media deserved, embarked upon a monologue that wandered with archaeological precision through the history and byways of chemistry, disclosing along the way that the paste consisted of ammonium

perchlorate (69.6 percent), aluminium (16.0 percent), HTPB polymer (12.04 percent), an epoxy curing agent (1.96 percent) and iron oxide catalyst (0.4 percent).

But Dr Proudhon was not finished with us yet, for he now revealed that the booster rockets constituted only a part, and perhaps not the most important, of the mechanics of propulsion, for the main rocket was in addition equipped with a liquid-hydrogen-and-oxygen engine to help it complete its journey into space. This masterwork of engineering, named Vulcain after the francophone-version of the Roman god of fire and iron, had been thirty years in the making and based its claim to greatness on its ability to keep two highly reactive and pressurised propellants safely separated in adjoining tanks, preventing them from combining prematurely and maintaining them at their different freezing temperatures (minus 251 degrees centigrade for hydrogen and minus 184 for oxygen) even when, just fifty centimetres away, the combustion chamber into which they were being driven by a turbo pump, at a rate of six hundred litres per second, was burning at 1,500 degrees centigrade. There were a thousand other things about Vulcain which might interest anyone seeking more than a cursory journalistic understanding, Dr Proudhon concluded coldly, but he hoped that we might excuse him: he was due back at his home in Kourou shortly, as he and his wife planned to take their children on a late-afternoon outing to watch the newly hatched baby turtles learning to swim in the Maroni River.

The pyrotechnician appeared imperturbable in the face of his power. He had at his command more force than almost any ruler in history, more – for example – than the eighteenth-century Chinese emperor Qian Long, a paper tiger by comparison, whose armies had viciously subdued both the Uyghurs and the Mongols. But Dr

Proudhon's strength was the opposite of intemperate might, it was the disciplined and sedated authority of the scientist entrusted with the safe management of unfeasible rage. Somewhere inside this white-coated man, there must have remained vestigial urges to dominate, shout, master, blow up and attack, but how carefully such instincts had been contained, by what cautious laboratory rules his urges had been governed, how quiet modern omnipotence could be.

7.

The satellite and its launch vehicle were practical achievements no doubt, but they were also, and perhaps primarily, the products of revolutionary changes in belief systems.

Isaac Newton (whose namesake street was home to Kourou's only travel agency) was the first to postulate the theories on which the launch itself would be based, when he speculated that if a cannonball could be fired at a tremendous speed from a great height, the top of an implausibly tall mountain, for instance, it would orbit right around around the earth, for gravity would pull it downwards at the same rate at which the planet spun away from it. The Englishman's ideas, along with a raft of other discoveries in chemistry and physics, were the fruits of a scientific perspective that had marked a gradual separation in European consciousness from the long and tenebrous age of magic that had preceded it.

Four hundred kilometres from where the rocket was being readied, in the rain forest on the border with Brazil, lived the last of the Waiwai Indians. The majority of the tribe had long ago left the jungle and moved into towns or government-sponsored camps (one group lived in Kourou, where they ran the popular Waiwai takeaway restaurant in the Place de l'Europe). But those left in the wild preserved the rudiments of a cosmology comparable in structure to that of the inhabitants of the prescientific West.

For the Waiwai, the movements of the planets, the cycles of the weather, the behaviour of animals and the properties of plants, were all apprehended mythologically, without any attempt at precise observation or detached understanding. There was no room for developments in knowledge. Time stood still. Traditions could not be altered or probed, being the preserve of sacred elders and medicine men. The Waiwai projected themselves into all they saw. Why might the moon be a particularly deep shade of red in the evening? Because someone in the tribe had developed violent thoughts, likely to break into bloodshed the next day. Why had it not rained? Because the network of anacondas who lived in the clouds and spat down droplets of water had been angered during a hunt. What was the sky? A clay pan resting on three upright rocks.

In the Waiwai schema, man could not directly affect the world. He would have to ask, or more accurately implore, the spirits responsible for its functioning. On a breathless day, he would have to take care not to injure any tapirs, for the wind was controlled by a giant example of one hidden in the sky, responsible for wafting a large palm leaf to create a breeze. If he wanted the sun to come out, he would have to put on a diadem of toucan feathers and blow down a long pipe carved with anaconda patterns, so as to flatter the sacred orb into rising into the sky.

The scientists now occupied by fuelling and loading in their hangars at the edge of the jungle had moved unrecognisably far from such thinking. They had completed PhDs on the numerical analysis of stirred-tank hydronymics and the drag reduction effects of polymer additives on turbulent pipe flow. They read the universe as an orderly and logical machine, which worked

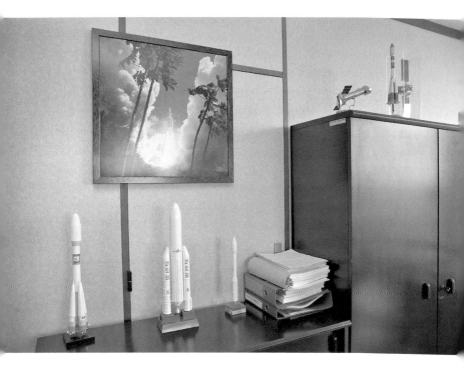

independently of their sins and virtues, a mere impassive clock, which could be taken apart by reason and rendered theoretically predictable without requiring recourse to incantation.

And yet, as a non-scientist examining the rocket-assembly building, gazing at a needle of solid propellant nine storeys tall, one felt that a most unmagical of approaches had nevertheless succeeded in producing a device which was not entirely free of supernatural associations. Living with science without understanding it forced one to consider machines in the same quasi-mystical way in which a sparsely-clothed Waiwai might have contemplated the phenomena of the heavens. What talent and insolence it was on the part of the white-coated fraternity to have succeeded in generating an impression of mystical awe with the help only of an ammonium perchlorate composite.

8.

Nevertheless, as the appointed launch time approached, a feeling of tension and of foreboding became palpable. The sky turned a purply-grey, and the air was oddly still. In Kourou, a France Telecom van collided with a car at the corner of the Avenue Nobel and the rue Mère Theresa. The lizards were out in force at the Atlantis Hotel.

The weather, always complex and histrionic in the region, was of particular concern to the scientists. Almost every afternoon brought a violent thunderstorm, with clouds up to eighteen kilometres thick, eight kilometres being the usual maximum over northern Europe. In tearing through such a lofty mass at great velocity, the rocket ran a risk of driving a lightning bolt into its own flight path. Furthermore, the area was known for its high atmospheric winds, which meant that even if all was still at ground level, thirty kilometres up, a tapir

with a palm leaf might be stirring up a current capable of deflecting the rocket onto a catastrophically errant trajectory.

At eight in the evening, an hour before launch, under armed guard, we were driven in the darkness to an observation site in the jungle, only three kilometres from where the boosters would be ignited. We took our places on a raised clearing with uninterrupted views onto the launchpad – and said little.

Technologically extreme situations have a habit of whetting the appetite for sentimental safety briefings, which in turn tend to reveal both the scale of the danger involved and the inadequacy of the proposed response to it. A member of the elite Brigade de Sapeurs-Pompiers de Paris – a branch office of which operated in the space centre – came forward to address our group. At this distance, a malfunctioning rocket would be upon us in under a second, the fireman declared, though this hopeless prospect did not prevent him from distributing a set of yellow gas masks and explaining that we should secure them over our heads to activate their breathing tubes, then leave them alone until, and unless, there was an emergency. Despite these instructions, a few minutes later, ever alert to the need to bring science to life, the Hong Kong television presenter removed her cameraman's mask from its casing and, with it hanging loosely over her face, delivered a muffled soliloquy to the camera, outlining the hazards to which she was exposing herself for her audience – while her own mask remained cocooned inside a tasselled Balenciaga handbag.

A screen had been set up to provide us with a live feed from the control room. At their terminals, a group of thirty were monitoring Ariane's vital functions. Dr Proudhon, back from the turtles, was at his desk, staring impassively at a bank of screens. In a challenge to the team's sense of their indispensability, a second identical control

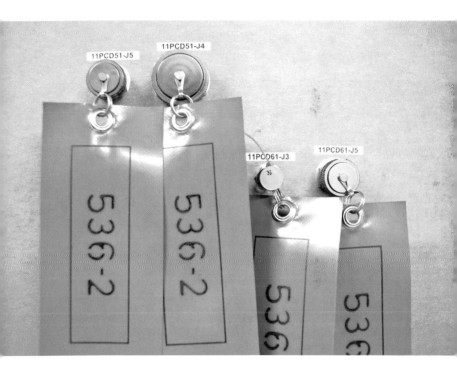

centre was up and running a few kilometres further away to the east, harbouring another thirty, identically trained people, standing by to pick up operational command were the launcher to get off to a temperamental start and incinerate their colleagues.

Across the humid night, Ariane stood out on its platform, illuminated by a set of arc lamps around which clouds of tropical insects were dancing frenziedly. Deeper in the jungle, there were peccaries and spider monkeys, giant anteaters and harpy eagles, while in this unlikely outpost of air-conditioned Newtonian civilisation, something was preparing to leave the planet. All shipping and aircraft had been cleared in an arc extending to the West African coast. Ariane's engines took their last breaths of oxygen through a thick black umbilical cord. Every remaining human had been removed from the area. It was hard not to feel some of the same sadness that might attend the departure of an ocean liner or the lowering of a coffin.

Thirty seconds before lift-off, Dr Proudhon's voice came over the loudspeakers. The tapir seemed ready to allow the mission to proceed. The work of years was about to condense itself into an instant. Time, which in so many of our mid-afternoons flows by aimlessly and languidly, felt meaningful at last. With ten seconds left, like a prison warder releasing his charge, Dr Proudhon turned a set of keys and initiated the formal count-down. There would now be no way for matters to end peacefully. *Dix, neuf, huit, sept, retrait des ombilicaux* ... It was peculiar to hear a sequence so indelibly associated, via cinema, with Cape Canaveral being enunciated in another language. At *cinq,* there was a dull sound as if a shell had gone off, and a first puff of smoke rose from the bottom of the launcher. By *trois,* white billows had enveloped its base, and on the cue of *un, et décollage* ... , the rocket ripped itself off its pad in immaculate silence.

When the noise reached us a second later, we recognised it as the loudest any of us had ever heard, louder of course than thunder, jets and the explosive charges set off in quarries, the concentrated energies of tens of millions of years of solar energy being released in an instant. We recognised that we were caught up in an irreproducible and irrepresentable event. Moreover, what lent the scene its particular drama, though it would invariably be omitted from later accounts, was our terror as to what would happen next, for it seemed unlikely that there could ever be a sane, bloodless conclusion to this cataclysm.

The rocket rose, and there was a collective gasp, a most naive, amazed *Ahh*, inarticulate and primordial, as all of us for a moment forgot ourselves – our education, manners and sense of irony – to follow the fine white javelin on its ascent through the southern skies.

There was light, too: the richest orange of the bomb maker's palette. The rocket became a giant burning bulb in the firmament, letting us see as if by daylight the beach, the town of Kourou, the jungle, the space centre's buildings and the faces of our stunned fellow spectators.

The launch seemed capable of upholding any number of symbolic readings. Here was a tube carrying an Asian television satellite into orbit, but it was also, depending on one's inclinations (and there was little in the scene to prevent such thoughts), a spirit, Yahweh, the Holy Trinity, or a reincarnation of Mawari, the omnipotent creator of the Waiwai universe. The scene brought to mind the moments of smoke and fire which the Old Testament prophets had invoked to make their audiences shudder before the majesty of their lord. And yet this modern impression of divinity was being generated by the most secular and pagan of machines. Science had taught us to upstage the gods.

The launcher pierced through a layer of clouds and disappeared, leaving only an untraceable roar which reverberated across the heavens, the earth and the jungle. Then, through a gap in the clouds, it promptly reappeared, higher up than any plane could fly and reduced to a smudge of flame. The satellite I had been in a room with just a few days before was already reaching the upper atmosphere. The rocket boosters had been jettisoned somewhere in between and were on their way down, halfway to Africa by now, swaying from parachutes.

An odd quiet settled over us again. A nature-made wind could be heard through the trees, then the call of a monkey. My mouth was dry. I realised that my left hand was hanging in mid-air, still fixed in the same position it had been in when the commotion began. Nearby, under a tent in which a few rows of chairs had been set up, two people were speaking quietly in French. A young woman with shoulder-length hair and an unaffected sort of beauty was explaining to a friend how the satellite would reach its final orbit. She had on a white cotton skirt adorned with small bluebells, and she was using one of her knees to represent the earth and a long, slender finger to trace the path of the satellite. She was keen to make clear to her companion that the launcher would not, as might have been presumed, deliver the satellite all the way to its destination; instead, its job was to lift it 250 kilometres into the atmosphere, to what was known as the point of injection, from where the satellite would require an additional ten days to travel, by means of its own motors, to its orbiting location, thirty-six thousand kilometres above Japan. It would need to complete a number of lower orbits in a curious elliptical shape (sketched across her skirt) before it achieved sufficient force to describe a perfect circle (around her left knee) – an intricate piece of ballistic science I was unable to follow to its conclusion, for the tensions of the scene grew distracting enough to force me to walk out further into the night.

Command of the rocket now passed from the engineers in Kourou to a series of ground tracking stations which ringed the earth, unbeknownst to the inhabitants of their host countries. The first of these was located in the middle of the Atlantic, on Ascension Island, where a small building was manned by a solitary technician brought over from France by ship a month earlier, whose one responsibility was to track Ariane's journey during the four-minute window following the ejection of its boosters. After that, control devolved to another, similarly lonely tracking facility north of Libreville, in Gabon, which in turn ceded it to a station in Malindi, Kenya. The last in the chain was a lighthouse in the western Australian desert, to whose isolation I felt, at that moment, singularly able to relate.

9.

A post-launch party had been organised in a beachside restaurant in Kourou. The dining room had been decorated with images of Ariane and its satellite, and a buffet laid out that included goat, octopus and a tower of barbecued shrimp sculpted into the shape of a launcher.

On the other side of the earth – where it was tomorrow already, though it had been only twenty-seven minutes since the rocket left our company – the upper-stage engine cut out, and Ariane's nose cone flipped up to allow the satellite to begin its progress under its own power.

There was high emotion, even euphoria, amongst our group. The Japanese executives pressed themselves one by one against the white shirt of the director of the space agency, the NASA staffers began drinking beer, the propulsion team uncorked some Bordeaux. I shared in their excitement. The planet's outer atmosphere, which

so few objects had ever penetrated in its four-and-a-half-billion-year
history (how quiet it must have been in space during the Roman era,
how uneventful the Middle Ages from 250 kilometres up), had just
let through our elegant white spear. The engineers had learnt how
to make a home for one of our machines in the most inhuman of
places. There would soon be another eye above us in the firmament.
I thought of Walt Whitman's 'Passage to India', from *Leaves of Grass*,
in which the poet had pictured himself surveying the earth and the
works of man and nature from on high, an imaginative exercise to
which only the modern satellite had been able to lend a concrete
dimension:

> *I see over my own continent the Pacific Railroad, surmounting every barrier;*
> *I see continual trains of cars winding along the Platte, carrying*
>   *freight and passengers;*
> *I hear the locomotives rushing and roaring, and the shrill steam-whistle,*
> *I hear the echoes reverberate through the grandest scenery in the world;*
> *I cross the Laramie plains – I note the rocks in grotesque shapes–*
>   *the buttes;*
> *I see the plentiful larkspur and wild onions – the barren, colorless,*
>   *sage-deserts…*

Now, in a garishly lit room at the fringes of the South American
jungle, a glass of Brazilian rum in hand, I turned against my ten-
dencies to pessimism and suspiciousness. It seemed too easy to
claim that there was nothing new under the sun, that any material
progress would inevitably be counterbalanced by spiritual regress,
that our spear-wielding ancestors had been as wise and good as ourselves and that the onward march of rational thought had brought

with it nothing but tragedy. Did any of these arguments take into account Ariane's profile on her way up? Did they credit the impeccable logic of her hydraulic systems? And most of all, did not such bromides merely betray the resentment of a defeated and unimaginative class? I felt my allegiances shift to the engineers and technicians around me, these new medicine men who often sported baseball caps, and had a tendency towards unsophisticated humour – but who had nonetheless mastered the workings of the universe. What astonishing creatures they were! What extraordinary horizons they had opened up!

The only person who seemed unable to join in the excitement was the Hong Kong television presenter, who sat glumly at a table pushing shrimp around her plate. She had found the launch a disappointment, she said and, smiling weakly, added that she had now started her own countdown: to her return to her apartment overlooking Victoria Harbour. Her bitterness smacked of bruised egocentricity. The only topic she appeared comfortable with was mosquitoes. Though tales of the bites of others are usually no less wearing than those of their dreams, she boasted at length about how she had been devoured during the launch, and proceeded to show off her ankles, hopeful that the interest of so many minute beings might stand as a last, desperate proof of her continued magnetism. I realised then that it might be possible to feel jealous of a rocket.

10.

I helped myself to some goat stew and sweet potato and made my way to a table outside. There was an improbable density of stars in the sky, as if glitter had been prodigally scattered across a swathe of black satin. For thousands of years, it had been nature – and its supposed creator – that had had a monopoly on awe. It had been the icecaps, the deserts, the volcanoes and the glaciers that had given us a sense of finitude and limitation and had elicited a feeling in which fear and respect coagulated into a strangely pleasing sense of humility, a feeling which the philosophers of the eighteenth century had famously termed the sublime.

But then had come a transformation to which we were still the heirs, and of which Ariane was an exemplar. Over the course of the nineteenth century, the dominant catalyst for that feeling of the sublime had ceased to be nature. We were now deep in the era of the technological sublime, when awe could most powerfully be invoked not by forests or icebergs but by supercomputers, rockets and particle accelators. We were now almost exclusively amazed by ourselves.

Nature, meanwhile, had become an object of concern and pity, like a former foe arrived at one's gates, bleeding to death. No longer standing as a symbol of all which surpassed us, the natural landscape instead everywhere bore the scars of our quixotic powers. We could look up at the diminishing snows of Kilimanjaro and reflect on the ill effects of our turbines. We could fly over denuded stretches of the Amazon and perceive the rain forest to be no more robust than a single flower in our hands. We had learnt to feel respect for circuit boards and pity and guilt towards glaciers.

11.

I had planned to get a lift back to the Atlantis hotel from one of the engineers who lived nearby, but at one in the morning, he put on a paper hat and started dancing with a Brazilian waitress, so I headed out alone.

The streets of Kourou, never an inviting milieu, looked especially drab and sinister this late at night. The shops were shuttered and largely unlit. The Waiwai restaurant, having been robbed the day

before by a gang from across the border in Surinam, was cordoned off with police tape.

I fell into an unexpectedly melancholic mood, perhaps inspired by the realisation of how few of the accomplishments that lay behind Ariane's launch would in fact be able to filter down reliably to every-day experience and hence how much of life was set to continue as it had always done, prey to the same inner inclemencies, gravitational pulls and depressions as those our cave-dwelling ancestors had known. Our bodies would disintegrate, our plans would be blown off course, we would be visited by cruelty, lust and silliness – and only occasionally would we be in a position to recover contact with the speed, elegance, dignity and intelligence evidenced by the great machines.

I felt keenly the painful psychological adjustments required by life in modernity: the need to juggle a respect for the potential offered by science with an awareness of how perplexingly limited and narrowly framed might be its benefits. I felt the temptation of hoping that all activities would acquire the excitement and rigours of engineering while recognising the absurdity of those who, overly impressed by technological achievement, lose sight of how doggedly we will always be pursued by baser forms of error and absurdity.

12.

The next day was my last in French Guiana. To kill time before my evening flight, I toured the capital, Cayenne, ending up in the nation's main museum, a traditional tin-roofed Creole house in a poor state of repair, filled with spears, colonial portraits and pickled snakes.

In a back room hung depictions of the country's inhabit-ants at work, across different periods of history. The first frame was of a family in animal skins peeling fruit; the second of some fishermen staring limply from the side of a canoe; the third of a horde of slaves setting fire to a plantation building. Finally, twice the size of the other images, in attractive Technicolor, came a picture of five white-coated engineers attending to a satellite's cabling in a hangar in the space centre. The moral was clear: French Guiana had overcome the degrading labour of its past and was headed towards a future consecrated by the hand of science.

Yet I felt the awkwardness of having to look up to rocket engineers and technicians as our ancestors might once have venerated their gods. These specialists were unlikely and troubling objects of admiration compared with the night sky and the mountains. The pre-scientific age, whatever its deficiencies, had at least offered its members the peace of mind that follows from knowing all man-made achievements to be nothing next to the grandeur of the universe. We, more blessed in our gadgetry but less humble in our outlook, have been left to wrestle with feelings of envy, anxiety and arrogance that follow from having no more compelling repository of veneration than our brilliant, precise, blinkered and morally troubling fellow human beings.

13.

A little more than a week after my return home, the Lockheed Martin satellite successfully entered its orbit, joining the hundreds of others which necklace the earth. It now beams down images of WOWOW TV's programmes across Japan, from where it can sometimes be seen on a clear night, impersonating one of nature's stars.

VI

Painting

1.

Stephen Taylor has spent much of the last two years in a wheat field
in East Anglia repeatedly painting the same oak tree under a range
of different of lights and weathers. He was out in two feet of snow
last winter and this summer, at three in the morning, he lay on his
back tracing the upper branches of the tree by the light of a solstice
moon.

On a typical summer's day, this unknown middle-aged artist
is loading his car, ready for work, by seven in the morning. He
lives in a dilapidated terraced house in the centre of Colchester,
a town of one hundred thousand inhabitants, ninety kilometres
north-east of London. His sagging, dented Citroën has reached a
stage of decrepitude so advanced that it seems set for immortality. Across the back seats, strewn as if the vehicle had just been
involved in a head-on collision, are canvases, easels, insect repel-
lant, old sandwiches, a bag of brushes and a box of paints. There
is also a suitcase jammed with scarves and jumpers, for outdoor
painters tend to know the story of how Cézanne caught a chill one
morning while painting a sparrow in a field in Aix-en-Provence
– and was dead by sunset.

The road out of Colchester leads Taylor past a fractured landscape of warehouses and building sites. The commuter traffic is
impatient and quick to anger. Near the train station, an old crab-
apple tree stands in the middle of a roundabout, an unlikely survivor
of the roadworks which made off with its fellows. Eight miles west
of town, Taylor turns off the main road and starts down a little-used
farm track. Waist-high stalks bow and disappear beneath the front
bumper, like hair through a comb. Taylor finds his usual parking
place and, fifteen metres from the tree, arranges his base camp in a
clearing in the wheat.

The oak is estimated to be 250 years old. It was therefore already home to skylarks and starlings when Jane Austen was a baby and George III the ruler of the American colonies.

2.

To those familiar with paintings as polished, fully realised objects hanging in museums, it comes as a surprise to see the sheer mass of bulky, soiled equipment required for their creation. Taylor owns more than a hundred species of brushes including hog's hair ones with filbert tips, sable points, round heads, shaving brushes, soft Japanese watercolour brushes and handmade badger blenders.

Next to these, Taylor sets down a no less heterogeneous assortment of gnarled tubes of paint, which together make up his visual alphabet. It is hard to believe that these ingredients could be combined to create meticulously detailed skylarks, spring leaves and lichen-coated branches. Pastes which in lesser hands would end up as mud will be tamed and recast to take on the guise of facets of the earth and sky.

In time, there will be no reminders of the fleshly origins of painting. The dark magenta stains on the artist's fingers, the red speckles on his shoes, the glutinous green and blue smears on his palettes – all of these will be dissolved away, leaving the paintings to stand by themselves, as silent about their material parentage as a newly laid-out country road. To watch Taylor at work is to be reminded that even Perugino and Mantegna, usually known only as disembodied names in histories of European art, were once corporeal beings who dabbed paint onto bits of wood using sticks tipped with pig's bristles, and at the end of the day returned home from their studios stained by the tints they had used to fashion the cottony clouds which float serenely above the heads of their infant Christs.

3.

Taylor sets to work on the lower left-hand branches of a tree study he began a week ago. Between thumb and forefinger, he manipulates a sable brush, dipping its tip into a tear of magenta and raw sienna oil which will later, seen from a distance, coagulate into a perfect implication of a leaf in the noonday sun. Two hawks fly high above the field, on the lookout for rabbits stirring in the wheat.

The daughters of the local bourgeoisie, who often ride their horses down the lane which runs alongside the tree, tend to glance away from this unkempt artist as he moves around at his easel, though by way of compensation, there is always a sympathetic nod from a tramp who wanders the area, his trousers held up by a length of rope, shouting passionate obscenities against a government which dissolved a decade before.

Taylor first came across the tree five years ago, when he was out for a walk in the countryside following the death of his girlfriend. After stopping to rest against the fence which runs beside it, he was overpowered by a feeling that *something* in this very ordinary tree was crying out to be set down in paint, and that if he could only do it justice, his life would in indistinct ways be redeemed, and its hardships sublimated.

It is not unusual for Taylor to forget to eat while he is working. At these times, he is nothing but a mind and a hand moving across a square of canvas. Past and future disappear as he is consumed by the tasks of mixing paint, checking its colour against the world and settling it into its assigned place in a grid. An insect may crawl unmolested across his hand or take up temporary residence on his ear or neck. There is no more ten in the morning, no more July, but only the tree before him, the clouds above, the sun slowly traversing the sky and the small gap between one branch and another, whose

The tree from a glider at 1,000 feet

resolution and completion will constitute a whole day's work.

Taylor is tormented by a sense of responsibility for the appearance of things. He can be kept awake at night by what he sees as an injustice in the colour of wheat or an uneasy fault line between two patches of sky. His work frequently puts him in a tense, silent mood, in which he can be seen walking the streets of Colchester. His concerns are difficult for others to feel sympathetic about, however, for few of us are primed to feel generous towards a misery caused by a pigment incorrectly applied across an unremunerative piece of stretched cloth.

His progress is slow: he can spend five months on a canvas measuring twenty centimetres square. But his painstaking approach is in truth the legacy of over twenty years of research. It took him three years just to determine how best to render the movement of wheat in a gust of wind, and even longer to become proficient in colour. Whereas a decade ago he would have used at least ten shades of green to paint the tree's foliage, he now relies on only three, and yet his leaves appear all the more luxuriantly dense and mobile for this reduction in complexity.

Taylor found his teachers on museum walls. The great dead masters are generous instructors: it is not uncommon for one of them to impart a piece of technical wisdom to a pupil born five centuries after him. Works which ordinary gallery visitors might regard as inert entertainment are, for artists, living prescriptions.

It was Titian's *Man with a Quilted Sleeve* (1510) that taught Taylor how to paint leaves. It was not even the whole painting that engaged his attention during the hundred hours he spent in front of it in the National Gallery in London. He had no particular interest in the man's face; what detained him was the blue sleeve and, more specifically, the way Titian succeeded in suggesting an expanse of fabric at

once weighty and airy, despite working with a minimum of colours. Titian taught Taylor about economy, about how to imply things rather than explain them. He taught him that a painting of a tree should be the story not of each individual leaf but of the dynamic mass of the whole. There are only five blues in Titian's sleeve; the genius lies in the careful choice and judicious combination of these hues, so that while the lower folds appear flattened and empty, the upper ones manifest the presence of an arm so clearly that a viewer might almost think it possible to reach into the painting and grasp its bulk.

4.
Taylor defines Titian's place in the pantheon with the greatest compliment he knows: the artist was able to look at a piece of clothing as if he had never seen its like before.

Precise delineation is central to Taylor's conception of painting. The sky is never simply blue, he explains. In the region nearest the sun, at the top of a canvas, he uses ultramarine, to which he adds increasing amounts of turquoise as his brush descends towards the earth. At 25 degrees, he mixes in small amounts of nickel yellow and magenta until, at the horizon, there is nothing left but a soft white haze.

Taylor accepts the restricted nature of the challenge he has set himself. An essay he wrote to accompany an exhibition of half a decade of painting opened with the following declaration: 'For most of my adult life, I have worked on certain observations of the physical world. In particular, for the last ten years, I have been interested in changes of light as you look towards and away from the sun' – a summation of ambition finely poised between self-deprecation and megalomania.

The year before, for two weeks of a wet January, Taylor stretched himself out on waterproof covers at the foot of his oak tree and sketched studies of leaves, sticks, grasses, worms and insects. Some 180,000 leaves fell from the oak that winter, destined to be eaten, at an imperceptibly leisurely rate, by hundreds of millions of bacteria living around its roots. Taylor painted the grey-brown habitat of springtails, rotifers, eelworms, earthworms, millipedes, false scorpions, slugs and snails. He undertook a close study of lichen overspreading a bit of bark, having been drawn to the fungus after learning of its status as an epiphyte   that is, an organism which grows upon something else without feeding on it. He observed a stalk of goosegrass, a tall green plant known to naturalists as *galium aparine*, whose leaves concluded in minuscule hooks coated in cuckoo-spit, a viscous secretion produced by froghopper nymphs to protect themselves against predators while they suck their host's sap.

The specialised vocabulary of biology is dear to Taylor. It is a sign of attention and of a community ready to honour details. Technical terms do not in his eyes insulate us from the natural world, they merely help us to cleave with greater fidelity to its most precious and discrete phenomena.

5.

It is the close of an exceptionally hot summer day. Taylor is outside in his field, preparing to work through the night.

The moon is rising above the nearby village of West Bergholt, a view which he spent four and a half years painting before shifting to the richer possibilities offered by a single tree. He is still surprised by how hard it is to identify the precise moment when the moon makes its appearance in the sky. At first, it hides amidst the lights of faraway towns, and from there moves surreptitiously into

position – a small but powerful dot, beginning now to blaze – just above a distant wood. As it ascends, it undergoes a steady chromatic transformation, starting off a purple-orange, then ten minutes later losing its magenta flush, and at last, against an increasingly black sky, bleaching from yellow to a dazzling pure white.

Slowly, Taylor's eyes adjust to the gloom. The preponderance of green in the night sky makes him feel as if he were inside an aquarium. A lamp switches on in a house a few miles away. A star, orange-fuchsia in colour, appears on the horizon as the trees below sway in the breeze, like clusters of coral in an underwater current. Taylor turns on a pocket-sized torch which he has hung around his neck, throwing light onto his box of paints and his easel.

As the night wears on, the human world gradually recedes, leaving Taylor alone with insects and the play of moonlight on wheat. He sees his art as born out of, and hoping to inspire, reverence for all that is unlike us and exceeds us. He never wanted to paint the work of people, their factories, streets, or electricity circuit boards. His attention was drawn to that which, because we did not build it, we must make a particular effort of empathy and imagination to understand, to a natural environment that is uniquely unpredictable, for it is literally unforeseen. His devoted look at a tree is an attempt to push the self aside and recognise all that is other and beyond us – starting with this ancient-looking hulk in the gloom, with its erratic branches, thousands of stiff little leaves and remarkable lack of any direct connection to the human drama.

6.
Studio may be too grand a word to describe a small annex to the bedroom on the first floor of Taylor's house covered in studies of the oak tree at various times of day and year.

Despite its diminutive size, it is a particularly pleasant room. There are few jobs in which years' worth of labour can be viewed in a quick scan of four walls and even fewer opportunities granted to us to gather all our intelligence and sensitivity in a single place. Our exertions generally find no enduring physical correlatives. We are diluted in gigantic intangible collective projects, which leave us wondering what we did last year and, more profoundly, where *we* have gone and quite what we have amounted to. We confront our lost energies in the pathos of the retirement party.

How different everything is for the craftsman who transforms a part of the world with his own hands, who can see his work as emanating from his being and can step back at the end of a day or lifetime and point to an object – whether a square of canvas, a chair or a clay jug – and see it as a stable repository of his skills and an accurate record of his years, and hence feel collected together in one place, rather than strung out across projects which long ago evaporated into nothing one could hold or see.

Taylor knows that he is creating things which exceed him. He has a chance to get himself right on the canvas in a way that he cannot in the run of his ordinary life. He is not always the perceptive, patient observer. His social self is beset by frailties. He is nervous around others and apt to mask his anxieties behind an exaggerated laugh. Nor is he conventionally powerful. His journey has been dogged by peculiarly English discomforts. Achievements which might in other countries have come more easily – leaving behind a provincial, working-class background and asserting his artistic identity in cultural and intellectual circles – have been hard won and remain fragile.

Yet when he is at his easel, he can, without arousing any impression of arrogance, say that he knows how to paint. At such moments,

his peers are no longer just his drinking companions from the local pubs, and he himself is not merely the penniless son of a postman and a shop assistant; he is the confidant and heir of Titian.

7.

In the spring, after three years of work, Taylor helps a driver load up a van with thirty-two studies of the oak tree. Their destination is an art gallery at the edge of the City of London, where large commercial towers abruptly give way to irregularly shaped streets lined with small offices and shops. The paintings will be hung on the walls of the gallery's ground and basement floors, while the large plate-glass window facing the pavement will play host to a single twelve-centimetre-high canvas depicting the tree in early autumn.

The oak looks oddly foreign in this hard landscape, with its crowds heading brusquely for their offices, its cranes looming high above and its planes crossing overhead on their way to airports to the east and west. There are people out buying coffee, sandwiches, papers or new heels for their shoes, servicing their essential and practical requirements. In the midst of such activity, it seems logical enough to ask exactly what Taylor's art might be *for*.

To help us to notice what we have already seen. The tree paintings endeavour to excite and command our attention. They are in a sense comparable to advertising billboards, though instead of forcing us to focus on a specific brand of margarine or discounted airline fares, they incite us to contemplate the meaning of nature, the yearly cycles of growth and decay, the intricacies of the vegetal and animal realms, our lost connection with the earth and the redemptive powers of modest dappled things. We might define art as anything which pushes our thoughts in important yet neglected directions.

Nevertheless, Taylor is suspicious of any attempt to summarise art in words. He insists that a worthy painting will automatically render all commentary inadequate, because it must influence and affect our senses rather than our logical faculties. To convey the particularity of artistic work, he quotes Hegel's definition of painting and music as genres dedicated to the 'sensuous presentation of ideas'. We require such 'sensuous' arts, Hegel suggested, because many important truths will impress themselves upon our consciousness only if they have been moulded from sensory, emotive material. We may, for example, need a song to alert us in a visceral way to the importance of forgiving others, a notion to which we might previously have assented purely in a rote and stagnant way after reading of it in a political tract – just as it may only be in front of a successful painting of an oak tree that we are in any position to feel, as opposed dutifully to accept, the significance of the natural world.

The great works of art have about them the quality of a reminder. They fix that which is fugitive: the cooling shadow of an oak on a windless, hot summer afternoon; the golden-brown tint of leaves in the early days of autumn; the stoical sadness of a bare tree glimpsed from a train, outlined against a heavy grey sky. At the same time, it is forgotten aspects of our own psyches to which paintings can seem mysteriously conjoined. It can be our unspoken longings that surprise us in the trees, and our adolescent selves that we recognise in the hazy tint of a summer sky.

8.
Sales in the gallery are slow over the next eight weeks. There are no reviews in the national press. It is hard to buy paintings when one knows so little about what prestigious forces think of them.

Still a few customers come in off the street, without appointment, responding to instinct. One tree is sold at lunchtime to a trader from Deutsche Bank, another to a printer from Bow, a third to a couple visiting from Melbourne who have lost their way to Liverpool Street Station.

During the last week of the show, the smallest oak of all, a mere ten centimetres high, made up of oil paint on board, is bought by a dentist from Milton Keynes. Susan hangs it in the living room, where it coexists, and competes for attention, with a television, a set of wooden camels from Luxor and Noddy and Tessie Bear's village.

Susan enjoys showing the work to friends. This has nothing to do with vaunting wealth or status. In a sense which is not entirely clear to her, she wishes to tell others that she is a bit like the painting. She has seen the tree before. It is the tree from her childhood in Somerset which she passed on her way to school. It is the tree she saw on cycle rides through the Durham countryside at university. It is the tree which stood in a field across from the hospital when she gave birth to her first son.

Like a modern, secular icon, the painting creates a magnetic field around itself, proposing a fitting attitude and code of conduct for its viewers. The ordinary business of the day normally intrudes insistently on the goings-on in the living room. The television is a jealous screen. Noddy rarely misses a chance to make himself heard. Yet occasionally, late at night, when the rest of the household is in bed, Susan will linger a few moments over the painting and feel herself subtly aligning with its personality and recovering thereby an amplified sense of her history and humanity.

9.

The show comes to a close. Backdated across two years, Taylor has earnt the equivalent of the annual salary of an unsuccessful plumber. There is an impractical side of human nature particularly open to making sacrifices for the sake of creating objects that are more graceful and intelligent than we normally manage to be.

Taylor is undaunted by his fortunes. He has recently visited a village north of Colchester to look at a tributary of the River Colne. He wants his next project to be about water. He plans to set up his base on a jetty where he will, over a number of years, paint the river in a range of its moods and lights.

'Have you ever noticed water?' he asks. 'Properly noticed it, I mean – as if you had never seen it before?'

VII

Transmission Engineering

1.

At the wedding reception of my wife's youngest cousin, I fell into conversation with an affable middle-aged man who worked for a power company in Scotland. While eating chocolate mousse at a table near the dance floor, we talked of our respective professions and Ian told me that it was his job to install electricity pylons in the Scottish countryside, deciding not only on their location but also specifying their height, size and strength.

In his spare time, he was a founding member of the Pylon Appreciation Society, a group which, despite its meagre resources and frequent opprobrium, organised walks along power lines and looked forward to a time when curiosity about electricity transmission would be granted a place in the pantheon of legitimate interests. With three other members of the society, he had recently undertaken a trip to Japan, where he had been amazed by the nimbleness of the lines strung in the higher wooded valleys west of Tokyo. He had visited South Africa the previous year, where, he said, many pylons were of a highly unusual construction, or at least could seem so to European or American eyes. He described one pylon near Johannesburg which, with wide-open arms, no identifiable base and connectors fixed at a diagonal, matched none of my existing notions of how a transmission tower might be shaped.

Ian pointed out that whereas our culture openly invites us to be aware of birds and historic churches, it places no comparable emphasis on pylons, despite the fact that that they often rival, for ingenuity and beauty, many of the more established objects of our curiosity. He cited as an example Loch Awe in Scotland, a famously picturesque and romantic tourist destination dominated by the ruins of the fourteenth-century Kilchurn Castle, whose grounds are nevertheless crossed by a run of 400-kilowatt pylons linking the hydroelectric power station at Ben Cruachan with the Glasgow suburbs. On postcards of the loch and its castle, however, the electricity lines are almost invariably airbrushed out, so that the scenery pretends to a fictitious innocence, the bare hills and unsullied lake being symptomatic of what Ian (having grown increasingly garrulous under the influence of brandy) condemned as the garden-gnome mentality of sentimental Luddites.

2.

We exchanged addresses, and I largely forgot about our meeting. Then, eight months later, Ian dropped me a note to say that he was planning to visit England for a working holiday, in order to trace the route of one of the United Kingdom's most important power lines, a circuit responsible for providing the capital with two thirds of its peak-time electricity requirement, and connected at one end to a nuclear plant on the Kent coast and at the other to a substation in East London. He would be travelling on foot and by car and wondered if I might like to join him.

So we met at dawn on a glacial midwinter morning, at one side of the nuclear plant that dominates Dungeness beach. We were both warmly dressed, and carried sandwiches and chocolate in our rucksacks. Despite the early hour, the station was at an apex of activity, poised to fulfil the imminent demands of five million kettles and boilers. Some 750,000 years after our species first mastered the use of fire, the nuclear reactor represented our most advanced and cerebral attempt to keep the darkness at bay. It was generating 1,110 megawatts of electricity, yet emitting nothing but a high-pitched hum, appearing to be fuelled – unlike its untidy equivalents in coal and oil – by little more than the impenetrable and immaculate logic of advanced physics and chemistry.

Nevertheless, it was in a worrying state. Much of its exposed piping was rusting in the sea air, and a large cloth had been used to bandage up the base of a cooling tower. It seemed a particular folly that the English had been allowed to involve themselves with fission technology, for what people could be less appropriate to toil in this precise and rule-bound industry, given their instinctive distrust of authority, their love of irony and their aversion to bureaucratic procedure. It was evident that the field should more wisely have been left entirely in the hands of the Teutonic races.

There were 542 pylons and just over 175 kilometres of line between Dungeness and the endpoint in Canning Town in East London. Ian and I planned to make the journey in two days, whereas the electricity, travelling at a speed of 300,000 kilometres per second, needed a mere 0.00058 of a second. In less than the time it took me to imagine that the four cables emerging from the side of the station were sending their energy through to the capital's butchers, antique shops and nurseries, they had already done so – a notion rendered all the more implausible by the barren shingle beach on which the plant was sited, where any reference to mankind, let alone a teeming city, seemed implacably alien.

3.

We began walking beneath the line in a northwesterly direction. Ian was pleased to note that it was being carried by the L6 variety of pylon, which he judged to be one of the most attractive varieties in the country, with legs which were widely splayed apart, a lattice structure which was only minimally braced and arms which tapered gently downwards as if to acknowledge their load, features which set the L6 apart from, among others, the newer, heavy-footed and thickset L12 model, towards which my companion bore a particular antipathy.

Ian drew out a pocket encyclopedia of the pylons of the world, published by a South Korean press, featuring examples in every conceivable size and shape, and which served to suggest that there are nearly as many tower designs as there are distinct human personalities, and moreover, that our eyes are in the habit of assessing these inanimate structures by some of the same criteria we resort to when evaluating our flesh-and-blood acquaintances. In different species, I noted varieties of modesty or arrogance, honesty or shiftiness, and in one 150-kilovolt type in ubiquitous use in southern Finland I even detected a coquettish sexuality in the way the central mast held out a delicate hand to its conductor wire. The unspoken challenge for transmission engineers seemed to be to fashion a pylon which would subliminally read as possessing much the same blend of psychological and physical virtues as one might search for in an ideal friend or lover.

Although I had been alive for a troublingly long time, I had neglected ever to step under an electricity line, so I was surprised to hear the intense noise it released, as though strips of tin foil were being blown furiously around a cavernous fan oven. 40,000 kilovolts were running along the line, sparking an excited chemical reaction in the moist air as nitrogen and oxygen particles split apart. The corona discharge, as the phenomenon was called, prompted Ian to think of his recently concluded fifteen-year marriage. He explained that it was to this crackling sound, under the line running between Torness power station and the outskirts of Edinburgh, that he had first kissed the woman whom he had been abruptly left by a month previously.

Ian told me that, on an early date, he had driven Megan to some pylons to show her that the air around them can be so charged with volts that it can spontaneously ignite a small electrical device.

He brought out a fluorescent strip from the back of his car and held it up above his head, the household bulb flickering into life as it drew invisibly on the airborne current, the fragile vessel of milky luminous glass lighting up the couple as they moved towards their first embrace against the inky backdrop of the Lammermuir Hills.

In the end it had been a lack of shared interests which drew them apart, Ian concluded, gravely and succinctly.

To shift the mood, he presently tilted back his head and called my attention to some small cigar-shaped cylinders fixed to the conductor wires at either end of the pylon under which we were standing. He told me that their inventor, George Stockbridge, an engineer from California, had in the 1920s observed that the length of cable which each pylon could safely carry was limited by the cable's tendency to vibrate dangerously even in light winds. It was Stockbridge's achievement to show that this movement could effectively be stilled if a precisely calibrated vibration was applied in the opposing direction a short distance from every mast. He had devoted a decade and, some of his colleagues later surmised, some of his sanity, in fabricating a tube consisting of two heavy weights separated by a spring, which resonated at a different frequency from the conductor and thereby ensured the stability of the pylon as a whole. There seemed to be few man-made innovations whose creation had not exacted a disproportionate degree of sacrifice and ingenuity.

As we continued, Ian informed me that our electricity line was composed of ninety-one strands of aluminium cable twisted together as in a rope, a specification which placed it at the more imposing end of the spectrum, minor loads being generally carried along by lines having as few as seven strands to them. I also learnt that because a cross section of a line reveals a configuration reminiscent of the pattern made by a cut through a floral stem, various thicknesses of cable are named after different flowers. A seven-strand aluminium cable is known as a poppy, a nineteen-strand one as a laurel, a thirty-seven-strand as a hyacinth, a sixty-one-strand as a marigold and a 127-strand as a bluebonnet. Our slow progress to London would unfold in the linear shadow of a cowslip.

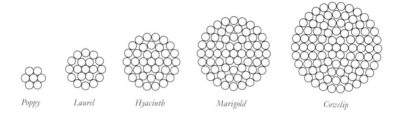

Poppy   *Laurel*   *Hyacinth*   *Marigold*   *Cowslip*

4.

Following the pylons meant stepping off the usual routes in order to wander at unorthodox angles through the landscape, over fences, through woods and under railway arches. We were reminded of the range of alternative networks which lie like a faded script under the dominant thoroughfares of cars and trains: the courses inscribed by water pipes, gas mains, fibre-optic cables, aircraft, Roman roads, badgers and foxes – axes that bypass the expected centres of interest and only announce their intentions through subtle or unfathomable clues, like a run of masts, some droppings or a grey box partially overgrown with ivy at the perimeter of a field.

At this stage in its journey, the line kept well away from humans. It was visible from rear bathrooms and garage windows. A glimpse could be had of it from the train to Dover, and from a bedroom at Pickney Bush Farm. Yet the pylons said nothing of where they had come from or were going, this mystery typical of a landscape

mottled with mute industrial objects, though one regretted how easily a placard could have been fixed to them, inscribed by a poet of modern life, who could, in a few lyrical couplets, have shared with passing ramblers some of the meaning and direction of this electrical peregrination.

In a swathe of dense forest known as Stockshill Wood, we came across a red estate car rocking forcefully of its own accord by a narrow path, and Ian remarked that the close observer of power lines must of necessity become a frequent witness to sides of human sexuality which find no easy expression within the parameters of our supposedly liberated society.

Sometimes we thought of death, for there were constant admonishments not to climb the pylons, though starker object lessons were provided by the many animals that lay electrocuted near the base of towers. Swans were empirically in the greatest danger, for an inattentive deity had located their eyes on the sides of their head, with the result that in the dark and in heavy fog they frequently crashed into the lines at full speed. It was normally only the leader of a flock who succumbed, the rest being warned off by the sound of a twelve-kilogram body hitting a cable at fifty kilometres per hour. Local dogs and foxes knew enough about the grid to keep a close eye out, sometimes lying in wait on moonless nights at the bases of pylons, where encounters would ensue between dazed swans, their heads severely distended, and frantic dogs who, fed up with the monotony of their tinned diets, rediscovered the ancestral pleasures of masticating on blood and feather.

I noticed that Ian often measured the distance between spans using an unfamiliar instrument equipped with a tracking wheel on its side, and that he afterwards jotted down notations in a leather-bound notebook. I spotted cream-coloured pages covered with

a latticework of algebraic equations whose incomprehensibility had the incidental benefit of freeing me to admire them from a purely aesthetic point of view, as the uninstructed might appreciate a musical score or a piece of classical Arabic.

$$T/T_H = \cosh\frac{wl}{2T_H} \doteq 1 + \frac{w^2 l^2}{8 T_H^2} \text{ and if } \frac{w^2 l^2}{8 T_H^2} \ll 1 \quad T \doteq T_H$$

Noting my puzzlement, Ian told me that he was calculating the force of gravity at work on the cable, and that in his equation l stood for the length of the span, w for the effective weight per unit of length, and T_H for the constant along the line. He explained that transmission engineers were unusually blessed in having at their fingertips a highly precise, efficient and universal vocabulary with which to convey even the most labyrinthine electrical scenarios, so that from Iran to Chile, ψ referred to electric flux, μ to permeability, $\mathscr{P}$ to permeance, and $\acute{\alpha}$ to the temperature coefficient of resistance.

I was struck by how impoverished ordinary language can be by contrast, requiring its user to arrange inordinate numbers of words in tottering and unstable piles in order to communicate meanings infinitely more basic than anything related to an electrical network. I found myself wishing that the rest of mankind would follow the engineers' example and agree on a series of symbols which could point incontrovertibly to certain elusive, vaporous and often painful psychological states – a code which might help us to feel less tongue-tied and less lonely, and enable us to resolve arguments with swift and silent exchanges of equations.

There seemed to be no shortage of feelings to which the engineers' brevity might be profitably applied. If only a letter could have been identified, for example, with which elegantly to allude to the strange desire one occasionally has to elicit love from people one does not even particularly like (β, say); or the irritation evoked when acquaintances seem to be more worried about one's illnesses than one is oneself (ω); or the still vaguer sense one can sometimes have that different periods of one's life are in coexistence, so that one would have only to return to one's childhood home to find everything the same as it once was, with no one having died and nothing having changed (ξ). Possessed of such a notational system, one would be able to compress the free-floating nostalgia and anxiety of a typical Sunday afternoon into a single pellucid and unambiguous sequence ($\beta + \omega + \xi \times 2$) and attract sympathy and compassion from the friends around whom one might otherwise have grunted unhelpfully.

5.

We walked on to Canterbury. The tourist itinerary advised us to have a look at the cathedral and the remains of a Roman villa, but we headed instead to a residential neighbourhood in the northeastern suburbs, through which the authorities, reluctant to let modernity intrude on the city's medieval skyline, had insisted on routing the cables. It felt peculiar to see pylons, which not many kilometres back had stepped magisterially across isolated forests, now landing in backyards and gardens and being co-opted into family life, like a stranger who, only moments after entering a house, is asked if he might help to carry the vacuum cleaner up the stairs. Washing was tethered to one pylon, a child's bicycle leaned against another. The electricity for Trafalgar Square ran over a group of deck chairs and an encrusted barbecue set.

Eight pylons later, however, the line was back in the wilderness. It bisected the vastness of Clowes Wood, then swung west towards the marshes of the Thames estuary. We walked for three hours in the rain until the line took us to the edge of the town of Sittingbourne, where we decided to stop in the hope of finding something sweet to eat. It was a place where, as often and inexplicably happens in small communities, everyone had chosen to enter the same profession – in this case, hairdressing – as a result of which most enterprises appeared to be close to bankruptcy. Luckily, we found a teashop advertising homemade cakes and what was termed an Old World atmosphere, and took our seats at the back. How cheerful one would have needed to be in such a place in order not to regret existence. A woman wearing a historically styled bonnet arrived with a pot of tea. 'I'll let one of you be mum,' she declared – which for a time prevented either Ian or me from taking the initative.

She disappeared into the kitchen, leaving behind what seemed to be her daughter, a girl in her late teens who, also sporting a historical bonnet, was sweeping the floor with an expression as distressed as it was beautiful. Despite the counterweight of two centuries' worth of romantic art and song crystallising the desire to escape the darkness of small towns, Sittingbourne remained for her an insurmountable foe, as stubborn as the congealed sauce which she was doing her best to wipe from the floor – her struggle representative of a greater, losing battle against the resistant forces of her life.

We drank our tea, paid the bill, and continued on to the town of Lower Halstow, where, as the evening tightened its grip, we took rooms in a hotel adjacent to a pylon. It was to be an uncomfortable night. Trying to fall asleep only served to confront me with an obdurate wakefulness, but any attempts to get up at once brought me face to face with a yet deeper exhaustion. At two in the morning, I switched on the light and took a formal decision to read until daybreak, so as spitefully to acquaint the wakeful side of me with the full consequences of its insurrection. Unable to concentrate on anything of substance, I looked in the drawer of the bedside table and found a panoply of brochures. They revealed that the hotel, which one could otherwise have taken for an aberration, in fact belonged to a chain with affiliates in thirty-four countries. Comparable charm and service were promised as far afield as Denmark and Venezuela, the entire globe seeming promptly smaller and more compromised as a result.

It was at least a relief to know that every one of these hostelries was connected to an electricity network. At that very moment, a sister hotel in Bucharest was drawing power from a station – probably the nuclear plant at Cernavod – to chill the minibars in its fifty-two en suite rooms. An inn in Uruguay was lighting its twenty-four-hour mini-golf course with current produced by a hydroelectric station at Salto Grande. And in the case of an Alpine lodge in the Tyrol, a pylon with a dense lattice construction had even sneaked into one corner of the brochure picture. I concluded that there were few troubling situations in contemporary life from which one could not distract oneself by wondering where the electricity had arrived from.

A storm began outside. The line became admirable out in the marshes, suffering the darkness and the North Sea winds with equanimity. A lone lamp was switched on in the garden, at the far end of a leaf-littered pool. It swayed in the wind, a satisfyingly obvious symbol of stoicism in adversity. I thought of the other signs which might still be illuminated across this part of Kent, in front of petrol stations, motels, pet-food suppliers and garden centres.

I thought too of our indifference towards the electricity network. The only humans truly in any position to feel grateful towards it were likely to have died a long time ago, in the 1950s, for it is rare to admire a technology which was already well established when we were children. The bulb is dependent for its prestige on a contrastive grown-up memory of the candle, the telephone on that of the carrier pigeon, the plane on that of the steamship, suggesting that histories of technology should usefully identify not only when a particular innovation was introduced, but also, and more interestingly, when it was forgotten – when it disappeared from collective consciousness through familiarity, becoming as commonplace and unremarkable as a pebble or a cloud.

It is hard to say when this stream of cheerless and increasingly nonsensical thoughts came to an end, but it was dawn when I awoke, slumped in an armchair, wrapped in my coat, with the copy of the hotel brochure open on my lap at an entry on a mountain-side hotel in Andorra, almost certainly powered by a hydroelectric plant near La Massana.

6.

We checked out early and regained our line. It was so dark that the day appeared to have given up on itself. Along the roadside, street-lamps flickered, their automatic sensors torn between respecting the hour and bowing to the implausibly low light-levels they detected.

Our line intersected with the route of the old Roman Road into London, but rather than heading directly into the capital, it instead meandered around the Medway towns of Gillingham, Chatham and Rochester. The horizon closed in. Settlements leaked into one another, creating a landscape without discernible beginnings or ends. We passed equestrian centres, schools of osteopathy and flower-bedecked roadside shrines to young men with oiled-back hair and young women with startled pleading eyes. There were boastful signs in shop windows – 'Bring us your quote – we'll beat it' – and

others which spoke with poetic concision of intrigues sufficient to animate an epic drama: 'Car wash: under new better management'. In a launderette in Chatham, we ate sandwiches to the comforting smells and rhythms of drying bed linen.

Next, the line passed through North Halling, and a mock-Georgian housing estate where Ian spotted that three of the houses had small brass windmills in their driveways. He was reminded of a Dutch book whose moral he often returned to: *De Schoonheid van hoogspanningslijnen in het hollandse landschap*, written by a couple of academics from Rotterdam University, Anne Mieke Backer and Arij de Boode. *The Beauty of Electricity Pylons in the Dutch Landscape* was a defence of the contribution of transmission engineering to the visual appeal of Holland, referencing the often ignored grandeur of the towers on their march from power stations to cities. Its particular interest for Ian, however, lay in its thesis about the history of the Dutch relationship to windmills, for it emphasised that these early industrial objects had originally been felt to have all the pylons' threateningly alien qualities, rather than the air of enchantment and playfulness now routinely associated with them. They had been denounced from pulpits and occasionally burnt to the ground by suspicious villagers. The re-evaluation of the windmills had in large part been the work of the great painters of the Dutch Golden Age, who, moved by their country's dependence on these rotating utilitarian objects, gave them pride of place in their canvases, taking care to throw their finest aspects into relief, like their resilience during storms and the glint of their sails in the late afternoon sun. It was works such as Abraham Funerius's *Het Bolwerk Rijzenhoofd te Amsterdam* and Jacob van Ruisdael's *Molen bij Wijk bij Duurstede* which had inspired the Dutch to accord decisive respect and aesthetic attention to their life-giving machines.

Ian concluded that it would perhaps be left to artists of our own day to teach us to discern the virtues of the furniture of contemporary technology. He hoped that photographs of conductors might in the future hang over dining tables and that someone might write a libretto for an opera set along the grid.

The line of pylons finally pierced its way into London through a discrete underbelly of ragged fields to the east of Swanscombe, and threaded its way through Northfleet to the banks of the Thames. There, beside a football stadium, the pylons ran up against their most imposing natural hurdle yet: a 1.3-kilometre crossing over the tidal river. To prevent the conductors from sagging dangerously over a span this long, three ordinary pylons would normally have been required, but a busy shipping lane precluded the sinking of piers, so the two pylons nearest the banks were left with little choice but to grow upwards, to a height of 190 metres, taller than a forty-storey skyscraper, their ruby-red summit lights barely visible through the mist. We felt proud to see a line which we had known for so long take a most grown-up of steps.

But there was to be no particular reward for this exertion, because once on the other side, the line was immediately driven into a landscape of warehouses, storage depots and cheap hotels, one of them boasting three channels of adult entertainment and a view of the Queen Elizabeth Bridge.

It was time for lunch and we thought of the food courts of the Lakeside Shopping Centre, but Ian pointed out that if we pressed on, we would find the line running against the edge of the bird sanctuary at Rainham Marshes. Owned by the Royal Society for the Protection of Birds, the reserve was an important resting place for migratory species, and had just opened a visitor centre, serving pumpkin soup and carrot cake, staples of cafeterias in high-minded institutions the world over.

Yet, despite a comfortable chair, an unimpeded view over the marsh and an extended perambulation, on the very balcony where we sat, by a common crossbill (an unfairly named bird), Ian fell into a dejected mood. Everywhere there were signs of the prosperity of the bird watchers' society: it had its own publishing sideline, it ran gift shops, it traded in tea towels. Next to the coffee machine, a large plastic robin with beseeching eyes urged patrons to drop money through a slit in its head. The organisation had seized on a minor occasion of individual gratification at seeing a bird and managed to transform it into a formalised and commercially robust activity, one which moreover tacitly claimed a distinct moral superiority over other leisure pursuits. It had done the archetypal work of culture: taking on an unformed, isolated interest and affording it a communal language and respectability.

How woefully immature the Pylon Appreciation Society seemed by comparison. It had only a handful of members, it had no cafeteria, it could barely afford to send out a newsletter. As a result, a sympathetic response to an electricity pylon remained for most of us a haphazard and unsupported impulse, an epiphany which might last for a minute on a drive along a motorway or on a walk along a moor, but to which no prestige could be attached and from which little of merit could emerge.

In an essay entitled 'The Poet', published in 1844, the American writer Ralph Waldo Emerson lamented the narrow definition of beauty subscribed to by his peers, who tended to reserve the term exclusively for the bucolic landscapes and unspoilt pastoral scenes celebrated in the works of well-known artists and poets of the past. Emerson himself, however, writing at the dawn of the industrial age, observing with interest the proliferation of railways, warehouses, canals and factories, wished to make room for the possibility of

alternative forms of beauty. He contrasted the nostalgic devotees of old-fashioned poetry with those whom he judged to be true contemporary poetic spirits, deserving of the title less by virtue of anything they had actually written than for their willingness to approach the world without prejudice or partiality. The former camp, he averred, 'see the factory-village and the railway, and fancy that the beauty of the landscape is broken up by these, for they are not yet consecrated in their reading. But the true poet sees them fall within the great order of nature not less than the beehive or the spider's geometrical web. Nature adopts them very fast into her vital circles, and the gliding train of cars she loves like her own.'

7.

Our line was running into problems. Whereas in the countryside it had often enjoyed straight runs of a dozen or more pylons, the increasing density of the city placed constant obstacles in its path. In setting down its feet, it had to bring to bear all the tact of a bulky man negotiating an object-strewn carpet. It tiptoed around gas storage tanks and railway lines, paused to make way for sewage works and crouched to avoid the wings of Embraers at City Airport. A few miles from central London, in an industrial estate which was home to a jacuzzi importer and a cake manufacturer, the line prepared to disappear underground for good.

There was, unsurprisingly, no fanfare to mark the moment, no acknowledgement of the chalk downs and the grazing meadows, the backyards of Canterbury and the geese of the Kent marshes. Before the power could enter London's circuits, it first had to be tamed by a series of porcelain insulators, whose convex, columnar forms recalled the ritual objects of the celestial liturgy of a primitive tribe. At the end of one particularly tall example, a single thick

black rubber tube, containing the steadied force of the entire line, slipped unceremoniously into a small hole in the ground, unknown to almost all of its five million end-users.

Ian had a train to catch. We confided to each other that we were unexpectedly sorry to say good-bye, feeling that we had experienced things together which would be hard to share with others.

In its new, modest incarnation, the line was now bound for a substation concealed on Shaftesbury Avenue at the rear of a Chinese restaurant specialising in Schezuan peppered duck. From there, its electricity would be distributed to the cosmetics counter at Boots on Oxford Street, to the cash machines of Tottenham Court Road, to the headquarters of British Petroleum in St James's Square and to a sign outside a club on Brewer Street advertising the services of a group of Estonians pole-dancing in the basement.

Along its subterranean course, the line would dissolve into ever smaller forces, from a prodigious 400 kilovolts to a more moderate 275 and thence, in the residential streets, to a placid 132, until it emerged from sockets, shorn of all impetuousness, at a mere 240 volts. As it passed, the current would perform the ultimate act of generosity: it would absolve its consumers from having to give it any thought, it would ensure that none of them would ever need to dwell on the idea of a run of steel-grey pylons tracing their origins back across the landscape to the southern coast, to a monolithic power station on the edge of a shingle beach, enduring the mutinous Channel waves and a corrosive wind while emitting a steady and ominous hum.

VIII

Accountancy

1.

Standing with your back to the Tower of London, looking across the Thames, you might notice a family of new office blocks lined up along the south bank. They took only six months to build – having been assembled out of steel frames sheathed in simple coats of tinted glass – and still do not quite seem to belong to the city, being oddly clean and impervious to the history which surrounds them, conveying a non-native sense of optimism better suited to downtown Toronto or Cleveland. Just to the east of them, in a plaza decked out with privately maintained trees and fountains, groups of foreign schoolchildren arrive by bus to take pictures of the river, while businesspeople, thrown off schedule by the rare boon of a punctual train or a clear road, sit on benches attending to messages transmitted invisibly to their phones through the luminous morning air.

A discreet logo at the top of one of the towers is the only outward sign of having reached the European headquarters of one of the world's largest accountancy firms. Despite such reticence, the building affords the inquisitive passer-by with notably unguarded glimpses of the goings-on inside. Seemingly more aware of having a view than of being one, the employees rest their besocked feet on boxes of printer cartridges, unselfconsciously consume lunch at the windows, swivel on their ergonomic chairs, stand in semicircles in obscure group exercises and write acronyms on white boards in rooms full of concentrated-looking colleagues – their behaviour unfolding behind triple glazing as if in an eerily silent film, accompanied only by a musical score of seagulls, river traffic and the easterly wind.

On entering the building, one encounters a lobby designed so that the head of any newcomer will ineluctably lean backwards to follow a succession of floors rising up to apparent infinity, and in the process dwell – as the cathedral-builders once invited one to do with their vaulted naves – on the respect that must be owed to those responsible for putting up and managing this colossus. However, unlike at Chartres, quite what one should be honouring is unclear. Perhaps hard work, precision, a certain ruthlessness and the surprising intricacies of the audit process. A plaque affixed to a wall declares, 'We like people who demonstrate integrity, energy and enthusiasm.'

To judge by the number of people seated on the lobby's red-leather sofas, it isn't unusual to be kept waiting a while for an appointment, surreptitiously to enforce an impression of the importance of one's hosts on the upper floors. A receptionist, no less aware of the solemnity of her role than a priestess at the Temple of Delphi, is on hand for a short initiation ceremony, handing you a badge and directing you to the sofas with a tenuous promise of rescue. There are free newspapers and bottles of water emblazoned with the firm's name. Waiting feels like the oldest of human activities, stretching back to the senators pacing outside the emperor's quarters in imperial Rome and the merchants lined up to see the caliph in the marble-lined palaces of medieval Cordoba. In the background, a bank of lifts emits random pings as security guards patrol the turnstiles, hoping for a confrontation to interrupt the tedium of their day.

As one does in a doctor's surgery, one may be tempted to look at one's fellow visitors and wonder about the problems that have brought them here. They are unlikely to be straightforward. The accountants don't cater to life's superficial needs. Their jobs did not even come into being until late on in the history of business, only after millions of people had gathered in cities and been grouped into industrial phalanxes – for, until then, accountancy merely occupied a few sporadic moments at the ledger by candlelight in a back room.

The advent of dedicated financial specialists, who are unable to fish or build a house or sew a coat but are entirely committed to answering questions of amortisation, standard engagement revenue and transaction tax, seems a culmination of a long history of the division of labour, which began in Ancient Egypt three millennia ago and, in oases like these at least, has generated spectacular returns and some distinctive psychological side-effects.

Everything in the accountants' building appears elegant and well-maintained. There are none of the cobwebs endemic to the ordinary world. People cross the corridors and elevated walkways with purpose. Five thousand employees are split into divisions headed Audit, Tax, Banking, Capital Markets, Real Estate and Risk Advisory Services. They are assisted by two hundred support staff who fix chairs, wheel biscuits into client meetings, reroute emails and clip together identification badges. A basement stationery store, stocked more prodigiously than Aladdin's cave, boasts a supply of three thousand highlighter pens, which could ring the earth in fluorescent yellow ink and which invite you to think of the many countries and situations they will run out in, for instance, one pen expiring in a hotel in Kiev, after covering the many salient points in a five-hundred-page document headed *Weighted Average Cost of Capital in the Copper Mining Industry*.

In the wider view of the public, accountancy may be synonymous with bureaucratic tedium, but from close up, this particular conglomeration of numerical talents presents the observer with a case-study of the discrete charms of offices, with their intriguing blend of camaraderie, intelligence and futility. The headquarters on the bank of the Thames is the setting for a range of behaviours at least as peculiar as anything that an ethnographer might uncover among the clans of Samoa.

GREEN BALLPOINTS

I resolved to spend time in the accountants' glass tower, as well as in one or two of their homes, in order to build up a snapshot of an average day.

2.

It is six o'clock on a late-July morning, in a village fifty kilometres from the office, in the Berkshire countryside. To define what is painfully coming to an end, thanks to the pitiless insistence of an electronic chirrup, as 'being asleep' doesn't scratch the surface of what has really been going on for the last seven hours, ever since one of the accountants I am shadowing lost contact with her conscious self while watching a regional news item and was transported off on the back of the swan of sleep. She may only have been lying under a duvet, in a room undisturbed except by the occasional sweep of car headlamps across the ceiling, and yet she was all the while being shuttled on turbulent journeys animated by unexpected faces and emotions.

She was back in the school gymnasium, taking an algebra exam and sitting next to a boy who was also, and without evident incongruity, a colleague from the Retail and Consumer Products unit. Then came a supermarket queue and the Queen shouting that someone had stolen her earrings, a scene which dissolved into a meeting on a ferry with a lover whom she hadn't seen in ten years, but who spoke of their break-up with an accuracy her waking mind could never have mustered. It is a wonder that we manage to be so outwardly docile, an arm or leg only infrequently stirring, while we travel on such ghost trains.

Once the alarm has rung, the accountant has little choice but to head for the bathroom without doing justice to her visions. Sentimental associations and impossible longings are shut down, and the self is reassembled as an apparently coherent entity, with stable commitments and a prescribed future. Yet in the haze of dawn, she feels for a few moments as if she still had a foot in both worlds, parts of herself holding on to the dreams as others soberly go through the motions with the taps and the toothbrush. But with time, the drawbridge to the night is pulled up, and soon all that is left is the noise of running water and, on a ledge by the window, a bottle of shampoo on which is printed in bold letters, in an implicit assertion of the supremacy of diurnal reality, the familiar yet peculiar phrase 'All-In-One Conditioner'.

How quiet the nation was only forty-five minutes ago, and yet how much hair-rinsing, necktie-tying, key-searching, stain-removing and spouse-shouting will occur over the next thirty, as the events in the accountant's house are replicated in a hundred thousand other homes within a gigantic circle drawn around the capital, from Folkestone to Aylesbury, from Haslemere to Chelmsford. Alarms are going off in Rottingdean and Harwich, alarms balanced on pine shelves and on marble-topped night tables, alarms which vibrate and others which set off the announcements of silky-voiced newsreaders detailing the trajectories of cyclones and currencies.

After showering and dressing comes a bowl of Crunchy Nut; then a scramble for a handbag and a raincoat for the walk in the chill air to the train station. Once outside, it seems extraordinary that the natural world should still exist and be so apparently undisturbed and serene, so indifferent to human concerns, with a new sky which has wiped away yesterday's squalls and holds no grudges, a scene of innocent beauty that bolsters any attempt to search within oneself for reserves of resilience and good humour.

The train will be on time, say the screens at the station, and the accountant walks to the end of the platform under Victorian arches spongy with the paint of decades, past advertisements for West

End plays and day excursions to historic castles. A plane crosses high overhead, a veteran of a still earlier departure, perhaps with a child on board at this very moment gazing down and seeing, within the circumference of a window, the full extent of the railway line threading its way from the coast to the city. Back on the ground, from a distance, swaying slightly from side to side, its headlamps on and sparks flashing around its wheels, a green-liveried train comes into view, sounding its toylike horn against a wide horizon.

Entering the carriage feels like interrupting a congregation. The cold air cuts into daydreams which must have begun far up the line and swelled across the wheat fields. The settled passengers neither look up nor give any other overt sign of taking notice, but they betray their awareness of the new arrival by dextrously readjusting their limbs to allow her to struggle past them to one of the remaining unoccupied seats. The train moves off, resuming its rhythmical clicking along tracks laid down a century and a half ago, when the capital first began plucking workers from their beds in faraway villages whose outlying farms had once marked the boundaries of their inhabitants' known world.

There is something improbable about the silence in the carriage, considering how naturally gregarious we are as a species. Still, how much kinder it is for the commuters to pretend to be absorbed in other things, rather than revealing the extent to which they are covertly evaluating, judging, condemning and desiring each other. A few venture a glance here and there, as furtively as birds pecking grain. But only if the train crashed would anyone know for sure who else had been in the carriage, what small parts of the nation's economy had been innocuously seated across the aisle just before the impact: employees of hotels, government ministries, plastic-surgery clinics, fruit nurseries and greetings-card companies.

Newspapers are being read all around. The point is not, of course, to glean new information, but rather to coax the mind out of its sleep-induced introspective temper. To look at the paper is to raise a seashell to one's ear and to be overwhelmed by the roar of humanity. Today there is a story about a man who fell asleep at the wheel of his car after staying up late into the night committing adultery on the internet – and drove off an overpass, killing a family of five in a caravan below. Another item speaks of a university student, beautiful and promising, who went missing after a party and was found in pieces in the back of a minicab five days later. A third rehearses the particulars of an affair between a tennis coach and her thirteen-year-old pupil. These accounts, so obviously demented and catastrophic, are paradoxically consoling, for they help us to feel sane and blessed by comparison. We can turn away from them and experience a new sense of relief at our predictable routines; we can be grateful for how tightly bound we have kept our desires, and proud of the restraint we have shown in not poisoning our colleagues or entombing our relations under the patio.

Familiar vignettes stream by outside: a power station, a patch of waste ground, a postal depot, a copse of ancient trees, a group of schoolgirls in grey-and-blue uniforms, a band of cumulus clouds spreading from the west, a shopping mall across a motorway, some underwear swaying on a line, and then gradually, the backs of suburban villas, heralding the train's arrival into central London itself.

At the accountants' building, employees are already beginning to course through the plate-glass doors. They have stepped off railway carriages at Victoria and Farringdon, London Bridge and Waterloo, driven through tunnels, been rattled by diesel buses, run down airport concourses, jogged across parks and cycled over hills and high streets, in each case hiding from the rest of the world the centre of the spider's web to which they were headed. What varied breakfasts they have eaten, too. Danish pastries, the remains of last night's curry, sausages, Scotch eggs and bowls of Cheerios and Coco Pops, jauntily named to lend their commuting consumers hope.

The employees proceed upstairs without looking around them. To feel at home in the office is not to notice the strange silver sculpture in the lobby and to forget how alien the place felt on the first day. The start of work means the end to freedom, but also to doubt, intensity and wayward desires. The accountant's ten thousand possibilities have been reduced to an agreeable handful. She has a business card which she hands over in meetings and which tells other people – and, more meaningfully perhaps, reminds her – that she is a Business Unit Senior Manager, rather than a vaporous transient consciousness in an incidental universe. How satisfying it is to be held in check by the assumptions of colleagues, instead of being forced to contemplate, in the loneliness of the early hours, all that one might have been and now never will be. She has a meeting scheduled with a team from an insurance brokerage in half an hour, leaving her time to buy a muffin and coffee from the cafeteria. The start of the day in the office has burnt off nostalgia as the sun evaporates a coat of dew. Life is no longer mysterious, sad, haunting, touching, confusing or melancholy; it is a practical stage for clear-eyed action.

3.

In a meeting room on the seventh floor, ten people have gathered to discuss the progress of an audit of a company in Birmingham which manufactures plastic packaging for the food industry. They range in seniority from a partner, in shirtsleeves at the head of the table, to a new recruit in an emphatically striped suit, who left university last summer. There is banter and affectionate teasing reminiscent of exchanges between a teacher and a group of cocky but respectful students. 'Watch the game last night, hedgehog?' the partner asks the young man to his right, whose hair is artfully gelled into spikes. 'Naturally, Robinson, but we'll wipe that smile off your face next weekend,' counters the latter.

Five junior members of the audit team have been in Birmingham every week for the last month, staying at a motel near the plastics factory, on the southern approach to the city. During the day, they have been working in the company's finance department, going over files and running data tests on their laptops. In the evening, they have frequented the Star of India, a Bengali restaurant located across the dual carriageway from Colditz (as they have nicknamed their accommodation). Travel policy stipulates that staff below the manager grade will be reimbursed up to £20.50 for the evening meal.

It isn't easy to encourage the accountants to expand on what they do. They feel that any curiosity shown by a civilian must conceal mockery – yet more of what they have been used to encountering from the wider world since they first announced their career choice at graduation. But with perseverance, their reflexive self-deprecation gradually gives way to a more earnest pride in their mastery of a labyrinthine craft.

I chat to Emily Wan. She is twenty-eight years old and a recent transfer to London from the firm's Shanghai office, where she found a place after graduating with exceptional grades from Jiao Tong university. She compares the audit process to a piece of carpentry. Capitalism could not function without her, she smiles. The procedures used for audits are identical the world over, enabling accountants to work seamlessly with foreign colleagues, as pilots might. The rules have been codified into a four-thousand-page bible, the *Global*

Audit Methodology, which I take to reading in bed. In Birmingham, every team member has been charged with substantiating a different aspect of the client company's balance sheet: one investigates its register of fixed assets, another its debt, a third its liabilities, a fourth its creditors and a fifth its provisions. At the close of the process, the senior partner will sign off on six hundred forms which legally underwrite the accuracy of the stated accounts – thereby enabling potential investors to have sufficient trust to let their money sail off on lengthy and intangible digital journeys in the company's direction.

At present, the team is devising ways to check the reliability of the VAT billing system. They are charting the flow of a hundred million pounds through the client's internal plumbing in the previous six months. Due to a missing file, there has been an irritating delay in the completion of a Non-Audit Services Annual Independence Continuance Form for Annuity Engagements.

Though the distinction between what is 'natural' and 'man-made' often dissolves on close examination, we are undeniably far from the human condition as it first manifested itself in Africa's Rift Valley 250,000 years ago. It is hard not to admire the dedication directed towards the small-print. Levels of commitment that in previous societies were devoted to military adventures and religious intoxication have been channelled into numerical needlework. History may dwell on stories of heroism and drama, but there are ultimately few of us out on the high seas, and many of us in the harbour, counting the ropes and untangling the anchor chains.

It is apparent that accountancy lends its practitioners a particular way of looking at the world. The accountants ask me not how or why one writes a book, but whether tax on a title is payable across a few years or must wholly be paid at the moment of publication.

They are like renal surgeons for whom one is first and foremost always a kidney.

More impressively, they seem to have no desire to undertake the kind of work which makes any claim to leave a lasting legacy. They have the inner freedom to exercise their intelligence in the way that taxi drivers will practise their navigational skills: they will go wherever their clients direct them to. They may be asked to deal with the financing of an oil rig one week, the tax liability of a supermarket or fibre-optic cable plant the next – without being detained by pressing internal projects and the pathologies and suffering these entail. They have no ambition to become known to strangers or to record their insights for an unimpressed and ephemeral future. They are well adjusted enough to have made their peace with oblivion. They have accepted with grace the paucity of opportunities for immortality in audit.

4.

In a ground-floor conference room, twenty-five new recruits are in their second week of a three-year-long accountancy training course. Last week they were given an overview of the principles of financial reporting, and this week they will be walked through the mechanics of company assurance systems. In an attempt to keep up their spirits, the firm has also bused them to an elegant hotel outside London to meet the chairman and to a spa for an afternoon of treatments and massages. They have in addition been introduced to the company psychotherapist, the in-house dry-cleaner, the director of information technology and the head of the accountants' gay and lesbian association, whose members convene for drinks on the first Tuesday of every month. And now, because the trainees have been listening to a lecture for more than half an hour and many of them

are showing signs of fatigue, the course tutor opts to release them early to sample a spread of croissants and Danish pastries outside.

For most of human history, the only instrument needed to induce employees to complete their duties energetically and adroitly was the whip. So long as workers had only to kneel down and retrieve stray ears of corn from the threshing-room floor or heave quarried stones up a slope, they could be struck hard and often, with impunity and benefit. But the rules of employment had to be rewritten with the emergence of tasks whose adequate performance required their protagonists to be to a significant degree content, rather than simply terrified or resigned. Once it became evident that someone who was expected to remove brain tumours, draw up binding legal documents or sell condominiums with convincing energy could not profitably be sullen or resentful, morose or angry, the mental well-being of employees commenced to be a supreme object of managerial concern.

The jobs in the world's glass office towers cannot be administered by the fear of an external power. Watchtowers are of no use in encouraging staff to engage their higher faculties in the drafting of annual tax deferment schedules, requiring senior managers to handle their charges with patient and costly respect. These overlords have been deprived of the cavalier attitudes of eighteenth century ship owners, who were enviably free to propel their slaves into the mid-Atlantic at early signs of scurvy. The new figures of authority must involve themselves with day-care centres and, at monthly get-togethers, animatedly ask their subordinates how they are enjoying their jobs so far.

Responsible for wrapping the iron fist of authority in its velvet glove is Jane Axtell, head of the accountancy firm's Human Resources department, based on the sixth floor. She recently organised a land-

scape-painting competition to help the auditors to release their untapped creativity, and is now, in an effort further to boost morale, engaged in lining the building's corridors and reception areas with plaques bearing the legend 'Our Values Statement: Who We Are and What We Stand For'.

There would certainly have been less for a diarist such as Saint-Simon to report on in Louis XIV's court had Axtell been present at Versailles. Thanks to her, the company now has in place a zero-tolerance policy towards bullying and gossip, a twenty-four-hour hotline for distressed employees, forums in which complaints may be lodged against colleagues and a tactful procedure by which a manager can let a team member know that his breath smells.

Underlying these innovations is the belief that workplace dynamics are no less complicated or unexpectedly intense than family relations, with only the added difficulty that whereas families are at least well-recognised and sanctioned loci for hysteria reminiscent of scenes from the *Medea,* office life typically proceeds behind a mask of shallow cheerfulness, leaving workers grievously unprepared to handle the fury and sadness continually aroused by their colleagues.

Contrived as the strategies instituted by the Human Resources department may seem, it is in fact their very artificiality which guarantees their success, for the laboured tone of away-day seminars and group feedback exercises allows workers manfully to protest that they have nothing whatsoever to learn from submitting to such disciplines. Then, like guests at a house party who at first mock their host's suggestion of a round of Pictionary, they may be surprised to find themselves, as the game gets under way, able thereby to channel their hostilities, identify their affections and escape the agony of insincere chatter.

There are, admittedly, few historical precedents for Axtell's job title or her professional lexicon ('client relating', 'personal branding') – a scarcity which may lead one to judge her as an unnecessary sickness. But this would be to misconstrue the sheer distinctiveness of the contemporary office, a factory of ideas dependent upon the ability of tens of thousands of employees to communicate properly amongst themselves in order to fulfil the needs of intemperate and exacting clients and so, by extension, an entity acutely vulnerable to internecine fighting, to the petty withholding of information between departments, to the nurturing of poisonous grudges over inequitable pay scales, to the appearance of dandruff on the collars of managers, to the splitting of infinitives in company releases and to the offering of clammy hands to crucial contacts – and hence an entity not above the communal salve discreetly embedded within karaoke nights and 'Employee of the Month' schemes, which reward their winners with river cruises and boardroom lunches with the chairman.

5.

For a long while, I try to meet this chairman, but first he is in Russia, then in India and then in the United States, though during this latter period, I am certain that I see him entering a lift at the London headquarters. Then he is for another interval officially upstairs but too busy to see me, until finally, I am allotted half an hour in which to talk to him about the future of the firm and the challenges facing his profession.

We sit across from one another in a bare room, chaperoned by the head of Public Relations, the purpose of whose presence is unclear, except to reinforce the implication that I should tread with care.

A show of surface geniality barely hides the chairman's impatience with writers. This morning, as on every other weekday, he was up at five, went jogging for forty minutes and was at his desk before seven. He rules over 12,000 people spread out across offices in Denmark, Cameroon, India, Senegal, Sweden, Scotland, Albania, Northern Ireland, Moldova and South Africa.

Yet despite his remit, he has renounced almost all the instruments and symbols of authority. He is universally known by his first name. He has no jet or chauffeur. He shares a secretary. He takes the train to work. He doesn't even have his own office. The architects designed one for him, with views of Tower Bridge, but he insisted on sitting in the middle of a regular floor at a desk no different from that of an intern. Its only distinguishing feature is a piece of laminated plastic, to the right of the telephone, on which is printed a quote from a speech by Theodore Roosevelt, in which the president spoke of the need for every man to strive for excellence and, 'if he fails, at least he fails while daring greatly, so that his place shall never be with those cold and timid souls who know neither victory nor defeat'.

The sight of the chairman's furniture brings to mind W. H. Auden's poem 'The Managers' (1948):

In the bad old days it was not so bad:
    The top of the ladder
Was an amusing place to sit; success
    Meant quite a lot – leisure
And huge meals, more palaces filled with more
    Objects, books, girls, horses
Than one would ever get round to, and to be
    Carried uphill while seeing
Others walk.

But Auden knew where leadership was headed. In modern times, he wondered,

> *Would any painter*
> *Portray one rising triumphant from a lake*
>   *On a dolphin, naked,*
> *Protected by an umbrella of cherubs?*

Of course, power has not disappeared entirely; it has merely been reconfigured. It is by posing as a regular employee that the chairman stands his best chance of preserving his seniority. His subordinates admire the sincerity with which he pretends to share their fate, while he privately recognises that only a convincing show of normalcy will prevent him from ever having to be normal again.

The chairman has also been forced to surrender his right to bark orders. He cannot scold graduates of INSEAD and Wharton. The one tool left to him is persuasion. Three or four times a month, in various corners of his empire, he therefore steps up onto a podium, takes off his jacket, looks out across an audience of three thousand accountants and, against a backdrop of Powerpoint slogans, tells them what admirable professionals they are, before adroitly slipping in a recommendation for improvements to their methods in the humble and supplicating manner of a preacher in an age of declining faith.

It is evident that success in his job will ultimately depend less on anything he might do than on his relative luck in aligning his reign with auspicious currents in economic history. He is like a general on a battlefield vainly striving to maintain an appearance of control amidst the chaos of sporadically exploding munitions.

Perhaps the chairman senses my concerns. He seems to regard our interview not as a chance to impart useful information but as a perilous test of his ability to avoid saying anything which might return to haunt him – in other words, to be as boring as possible. He persists in speaking to me in the same congenial but impersonal tone he might use to address a crowd. I ask him to expound on the company's future: 'No one is under any illusion that we face some significant challenges. However, there is no doubt in anyone's mind that we also have some fabulous opportunities.' What is his ambition for his employees? 'All of our people and partners want to be part of a winning, successful organisation, an organisation that is winning market share and is therefore growing opportunities for all of its people.' Does he like travelling? 'We are fortunate that we are already part of a successful global business, but we must do more to commit fully to our global organisation and the global market.' How does his firm differ from its competitors? 'Our people are our brand in our clients' eyes, and a differentiated client experience can only be created through our people living our values.'

After twenty minutes of this, I am tempted to ask when he was last troubled by his bowels in a meeting. But perhaps he speaks like this not so much because he wishes to keep secrets as because years of circumnavigating the earth, breathing conditioned air and head-lining conferences, have hollowed out his personality. It may have been a decade since he was left alone in a room with nothing to do. I feel my boredom turn to pity for someone who one might otherwise imagine had precious little to be pitied for.

6.

Lunchtime comes around, bearing with it a seductive smell of fried food which rises up through the atrium to the upper floors. Employees can look up the cafeteria's specials on the intranet. Fridays feature a 'battered catch of the day, tartar sauce and a lemon wedge'; Wednesdays are for curry; and on Thursdays there is a 'roast with all the trimmings'. To spare prospective diners any unanticipated delay, a webcam transmits live images of the queue.

However, not everyone is able to relax over the midday meal. At the very top of the building, in a series of executive dining rooms, senior partners are embarked upon the complex task of securing millions in fees from representatives of the country's largest enterprises, while pretending to be interested in nothing but their recent holidays and their children's education. Although the sums at stake here are incomparably greater than the ones dealt with by ordinary retailers or telephone salespeople who beg for custom in the soiled world below, the partners have learnt to adopt the serene and detached air of doctors or university professors.

Mark, the partner lunching in the east wing, perfected his approach during a training course entitled 'Delivery at the Client', the aim of which was to help attendees to develop their 'C' skills: Confidence, Commerciality, Communication, Capability and Commitment. The course was held in a hotel at the edge of a forest outside Northampton where, during an evening session, a pair of foxes peered in through a window at Mark as he sat at a table with his paper plate and plastic cutlery, while rehearsing the proper way to eat a meal with an imaginary client.

Now there is a real one sitting across from him called Arun, the chief financial officer of England's third-biggest manufacturer of dental equipment. The conversation is halting. The first course

has not even arrived yet, and the men have already covered cricket, Lake Como, Formula One racing, the relative ineffectiveness of solar panels and London pigeons. Mark is feeling especially tired today, for he returned home late last night from an oil-industry conference at the Marriott Hotel in Aberdeen, on the mechanics of using forward swaps and options to collateralise loans and advance cash flow to fund development costs. At least there is an impressive view out the window, and several more minutes can be devoted to sorting out which is the Lloyds Building. There is also art on the wall. The company likes art, and when it first moved into its new headquarters, it gave a firm of art-buyers a brief to equip almost every space with provocative and intriguing pieces by young artists. The dining room accordingly sports a large photograph of a cow who appears to be throwing herself into a muddy brown river. The setting may be India; the cow may be committing suicide.

Meanwhile, Guilherme is doing the rounds. Forty-two years old, from Bagé in southern Brazil, he has been employed by an outside catering company to wait tables during the lunchtime and evening sittings. He has in his day met with chief executives from the Axon Group, Braveheart Investments, Dana Petroleum, Indago Petroleum, the Omega Diagnostics Group and Zytronic PLC – though it might be fairer to say that he was in the same room with them for a brief period of time, for they are likely to have no particular recollection of this handsome, brown-eyed father of six, who once bestowed upon them a flour-dusted bread roll from a silver basket.

Today there is a starter of crab linguine, followed by a tuna steak with rösti potatoes. Hiring Mark to think on your behalf will cost you five hundred pounds an hour, whilst Guilherme can be had for just seven pounds – a difference explained not only by the history and relative prosperity of the two men's native countries, but also by Mark's three years of studying for a legal degree, a further two years spent at BPP college in King's Cross to acquire command of PAR (Principles of Auditing and Reporting), his membership in the Association of Chartered Certified Accountants and fifteen years' worth of graft, as he ascended from associate to partly qualified executive, from qualified executive to assistant manager, from manager to senior manager and finally from partner to senior partner.

Many months later, with the help of tickets to *Così fan tutti* and the opening of a show of Renoir's landscapes, Arun will at last respond favourably to Mark's carefully couched entreaties for money. For his part, Guilherme will have been unwillingly repatriated after the expiry of his visa.

7.

The period after lunch is strangely quiet, as if an ancestral memory of the siesta were muffling the normal energies of the day. On the seventh floor, workers sit at their desks, concentrated over keyboards and documents. Printers occasionally whirr into life, ejecting pages which give off the preternaturally intense and lingering heat of newly toasted bagels.

Defying the expansive regularity of the open-plan arrangement, where desks are identified only by stark acronyms like ML6W.246, employees have succeeded in imposing a subtle individuality on their work stations. There are family photos pinned to felt boards, and occasional mugs and trinkets honouring sports teams and holiday destinations. Crouching on the floor, one can see how many people have removed their shoes and are rubbing their stockinged feet back and forth on the carpet, a motion which produces not only the intriguing friction of nylon-rich fibres felt through cotton but also the impression of having in a minor way broken the rules and brought a hint of the intimacy of home into the working realm.

The office veterans are adept at domesticating their environments. They know where to hide their food in the communal kitchens and how to time their bathroom visits so as to reduce the risk of being forced into conversation over the sink with a colleague beside whom they have lately been seated in the redolent and tense atmosphere of a cubicle. Bursts of productive activity are punctuated by arrangements for dinner, updates on love affairs and trenchant analyses of the antics of film stars and murderers. How few are the moments of the day when money is truly being made, and how many are on either side given over to daydreams and recuperation.

Through the windows, people are walking by the river in casual clothes. Their leisure makes one wonder as to the deeper logic of the work unfolding in the building. However, large questions have a habit of feeling irrelevant when one is in the middle of an activity; one is simply preparing a document for a four o'clock meeting, or because André has requested it or Katrin needs it for a presentation in Bangalore. Then again, the accountants are experts at summing up the meaning of our working lives. The company derives the greatest share of its income from its employees' skill in preparing year-end financial statements which declare, following lengthy preambles about operational assets, capital receipts, loans and liabilities, that the whole point of a year may be summarised as follows:

	Current Year (in £)	Previous Year (in £)
Turnover	50,739,954	30,719,640
Gross Profit	**10,305,392**	**7,003,417**

Such numbers express a truth about office life which is no less irrefutable – yet also, in the end, no less irrelevant or irritating – than an evolutionary biologist's proud reminder that the purpose of existence lies in the propagation of our genes. The starkness of the year-end accounts only emphasises the extent to which generating money is really an excuse to do other things, to rise from bed in the morning, to talk authoritatively in front of overhead projectors, to plug in laptops in foreign hotel rooms, to give presentations analysing market shares and to yearn at the sight of Katie's knee-length grey woollen shorts. Long before we ever earned any money, we were aware of the necessity of keeping busy: we knew the satisfactions of stacking bricks, pouring water into and out of containers and moving sand from one pit to another, untroubled by the greater purpose of our actions.

8.

About those shorts: Katie is the twenty-two-year-old assistant to the head of the Northern European Retail division. Today she is putting together an itinerary for her boss's tour of Scandinavia in two weeks' time. She has a copy of *Discover Copenhagen* on her desk. She has booked him into a quiet upper room in that city's Imperial Hotel and scheduled a 7:30 breakfast with key staff from the local office, including Søren Strøm, Lasse Skov Kristensen and Morten Stokholm Buhl.

But Katie herself may be the only person in the vicinity able to concentrate on anything other than the captivating nature of her face and figure. So insistent and inappropriate are the thoughts that her beauty generates, it is easy to slip into a severe, impatient manner with her which may be mistaken for disinterest or even rudeness. Yet the company's code of conduct explicitly states: 'We have no tolerance towards sexual harassment in the workplace. Sexual harassment includes demeaning comments about a person's appearance; indecent remarks; questions about a person's sexual life; and physical contact that violates a person's dignity or creates an intimidating, hostile, degrading, humiliating or offensive working environment for them.'

Superficially, the code seems wholly and admirably concerned with championing the rights of innocent parties. There may, however, be a more cynical and less altruistic aspect to this unsparing paragraph, for what is really being protected is perhaps not a particular individual afflicted by indecent attention so much as the corporation itself. The feelings elicited by Katie's shorts are incendiary because they threaten to subvert the firm's entire rationale. They risk bringing to light an awkward truth: how much more interesting we might find it to have sex than to work.

There is nothing surprising about the corporation's jealousy. Every society historically has had to regulate the sexual impulse in order to get anything done. It is only our naive belief in our own open-mindedness which prevents us from recognising the extent to which an old-fashioned sexual repression has to be buried in our codes of professional conduct.

Yet equally, and paradoxically, such repression has disproportionately sexual consequences, for it is an essential feature of the erotic that it thrives most fully precisely where it is most forbidden. There were few places in the fourteenth century as sexually charged as the convents of the Mother of God, just as there are few settings today as libidinous as the laminated open-plan spaces of our corporations. The office is to the modern world what the cloister was to medieval Christendom: a chaste arena with an unrivalled capacity to excite desire.

If these two institutions have imposed harsh penalties on those who display signs of transgressive behaviour, it is because each is, or was, the locus of its society's most cherished values: the teachings of Christ on the one hand, and money on the other. Money is to the office as God was to the nunnery – and whether physical desire is condemned in the language of a sexual-harassment policy or in terms of sin and Satan, it stands as a comparable heresy, for it has dared to deny canonical goals, impudently implying that there may be elements more valuable in the world, and more consuming, than the stock price or the Redeemer.

The repression has paid dividends in one area, at least: logically enough, the office and the nunnery have been singularly popular in the imaginations of pornographers. We should not be surprised to learn that the erotic novels of the early modern period were overwhelmingly focused on debauchery and flagellation amongst clergy in vespers and chapels, just as contemporary internet pornography is inordinately concerned with fellatios and sodomies performed by office workers against a backdrop of work stations and computer equipment.

9.

The office starts to empty out at six, and an hour later, only those working on urgent presentations and reports are left, some of them facing a long night at their desks, punctuated by the arrival of Cokes and pizzas at around one in the morning.

The sun is nearing the horizon, throwing an orange light across the tower's glazing. What has been accomplished today? One employee advised a client on the tax implications of importing apples from Slovenia. Another wrote a paper comparing sales taxes in five West African countries. A third handed out name badges and logged in

three hundred incoming calls. These achievements will no doubt lose some of their significance with the perspective of time. Three years from now, the diary of the afternoon of the twenty-ninth of July will have become almost unintelligible, when it had once been sharply divided into pressing hour-long increments, devoted to appointments with colleagues whose very names and faces will have grown indistinct.

An employee from Advisory Services heads for London Bridge station and his commute back to Kent, stopping off on the way at a supermarket for a bottle of wine and a chicken breast in cheese sauce. He did not leave the building all day, for he was busy drawing up a spreadsheet analysis of an investment made by an American medical diagnostic firm and responding to emails from colleagues at work on a project in Denver. He is surprised, on stepping out of the air-conditioned atrium, to find how warm it is outside, how imme-morial the river looks, how many people there are alive, what varied sizes they are and demeanours they wear.

Exceptionally, the train tonight allows him half a carriage to himself. He has been making this same journey for the past twelve years. In the slanting summer light, when the smell of cut grass enters the windows from across the open countryside, he falls prey to feelings of nostalgia. He puts his feet up on the seat opposite and is carried back to other evenings which looked almost exactly like this one, which were of the same temperature and clarity, but hap-pened when his mother was still alive, before his children were born, when he was not yet divorced. He contemplates all that has been dif-ficult, unnecessary and regrettable but from a position of distance, with a calm and poignant vantage point over his imperfections and missed opportunities, as though his life were nothing but a bad sen-timental film and he its half sympathetic, half repugnant hero. He

has reached the age of reminiscence, though right now, somewhere in the scattered houses outside, there is a sixteen-year-old boy for whom this will be the one central hot summer of longing and discovery, the one remembered in thirty years on a train which is not yet made and remains as iron ore in the red scrub of the Western Australian desert.

The flat is quiet and guilty. Nothing here moved while, on the banks of the Thames, the accountant was meeting with IT and striving to keep his temper with an intern. He notices the bath towel thrown hastily over the sofa after the morning shower. The challenge lies in knowing how to bring this sort of day to a close. His mind has been wound to a pitch of concentration by the interactions of the office. Now there are only silence and the flashing of the unset clock on the microwave. He feels as if he had been playing a computer game which remorselessly tested his reflexes, only to have its plug suddenly pulled from the wall. He is impatient and restless, but simultaneously exhausted and fragile. He is in no state to engage with anything significant. It is of course impossible to read, for a sincere book would demand not only time, but also a clear emotional lawn around the text in which associations and anxieties could emerge and be disentangled. He will perhaps only ever do one thing well in his life.

For this particular combination of tiredness and nervous energy, the sole workable solution is wine. Office civilisation could not be feasible without the hard take-offs and landings effected by coffee and alcohol. The final approach will be made under the benign guidance of a Chilean Cabernet and the hypnotic, entirely untroubling retelling of the day's misdemeanours and cataclysms on the evening news.

IX

Entrepreneurship

1.

Towards the end of this project, I ran into an inventor (solar-powered electric scooters) who told me that no essay on modern work could be considered complete if it treated only well-established industries operating in orthodox and mature fields. He urged me to consider the legions of entrepreneurs, many working by themselves in short-let offices at second-hand desks, with only a logo and a business card for legitimacy, who every year bring forward unfamiliar inventions and services, in the hope of transforming our lives and their fortunes.

It was on his recommendation that, a few months later, I travelled to a convention centre located in an unfamiliar part of north-west London to attend an annual event designed to introduce small businesses to potential investors. Two hundred enterprises from Libya to New Zealand had rented stands in a hangar and were taking advantage of discounted accommodation in an adjacent Best Western.

There were new proposals in every imaginable sector of the economy: satellite tracking systems for cattle, hand-held radar devices for recovering lost golf balls, inflatable battlefield surgical theatres, high-density ear plugs for the spouses of snorers and a gift-voucher scheme for opticians. Many companies were rethinking ways of generating energy and fresh water. Three Swedes had brought with them a scale model of a power station run on chicken droppings, with supporting statistics on global faecal tonnage. Near the entrance to the hall, a group of psychotherapists were presenting plans for a service providing executives with psychological counselling on long-haul flights.

The range of offerings suggested that capitalism as currently developed remains in its infancy. We may think of ourselves as living late on in the history of consumer society, but the most sophisticated contemporary economy stands to be perceived by subsequent generations as no less primitive than we judge Europe to have been in the Dark Ages. It is a mere eighty years since deodorant was introduced, the remote-control garage door has been in existence for barely thirty-five and only in the last five years have surgeons discovered how safely to remove tumours from our adrenal glands and insert aortic keyhole valves into our hearts. We are still waiting for computers to help us identify whom we might confidently marry, for scanners to locate our lost keys, for a reliable method of eradicating household moths and for medicines which will guarantee us eternal life. Untold numbers of new businesses lie latent in our present inefficiencies and wishes. The fulfilment of a significant, and perhaps the most important, share of our needs remains untethered to the mechanisms of commerce.

2.

Looking through the brochure of attendees, I conceived a particular desire to meet Mohsen Bahmani, an Iranian who had invented a pair of shoes to help one to walk on water. Each shoe consisted of a spindle-shaped piece of fibreglass fitted with a miniature outboard engine, in which one could travel at fifteen kilometres an hour, while keeping one's balance with the help of adapted ski-poles. Bahmani had spent five years fine-tuning his product, testing it in the waters near his mother's house in the resort town of Mahmudabad on the Caspian sea, and envisioned application in both the recreational and military markets.

The two of us had made plans, via email, to meet for lunch at a Pizza Hut concession opposite the convention hall. I had just put in an order for some garlic bread and a bottle of sparkling water when I received the news that Bahmani had been detained at

Heathrow on the suspicion of importing bomb-making equipment and taken for questioning to an immigration centre in Hounslow. The message was delivered by one of his colleagues, a scientist named Mohammed Shorabi, whose old-fashioned courtesy, cadenced English and tweed suit pointed to a strain of Anglophilia now unlikely except among those whose contact with the United Kingdom has been restricted or exclusively mediated through literary works of the pre-modern period. Shorabi told me that he had, at least, managed to get Bahmani's promotional brochures through customs and had set them out across his stand. The two were colleagues at the Institute of Inventors, a research facility in Tehran set up by President Khatami in the hope of transforming Iran into a centre of innovation. Five of the Institute's products, the shoes included, were being presented at the fair.

Because it was already past one-thirty and I knew that he must have expended considerable energy in tracking me down, I asked Shorabi if he might like to join me for lunch. So we ordered a couple of Super Supremes and discussed Shorabi's own invention, a crash-protection system for cars and motorbikes. Based on exploiting what he termed mistakes in Newton's first law of motion, it involved the strapping of a system of weights and pulleys to the front wheel of a bike or the fender of a car. 'Nobody will ever have to die in a road accident again,' Shorabi told me, paraphrasing his company's slogan. He then pulled out from his suit pocket a sheet of yellowing newsprint torn from the *Tehran Times,* which featured a report on a successful test of his equipment conducted on a jeep at an army base in Mianeh – as well as, at the bottom of the page, an unrelated item about a strong finish by a member of the Iranian national ski team, Hossein Saveh-Shemshaki, at a slalom event in Turkey. Shorabi expressed regret that export constraints had prevented him

SHOES TO WALK ON WATER

from shipping a whole demonstration car to London, but he invited me to visit his stand after lunch to examine a child's bicycle which he had been able to bring over and which, he said, supplied ample proof of the principles behind his invention. Once back in the hall, he needed no convincing to ride up and down the carpeted aisles, his frame awkwardly hunched over a diminutive machine which reminded me of my own childhood Chopper bike, whilst talking rapidly in precisely enunciated yet increasingly incomprehensible English about automotive safety and what he alleged to be the CIA-instigated boycott of his innovations by all the major Western car manufacturers.

A few stands away from the Iranians, I met Caroline Oakley, a young mother from Kent and the inventor of the Crisp Bar, comprising twelve centimetres of grey-hued deep-fried crisps – as many as might ordinarily be found in a twenty-five-gram bag – pressed together into one oleaginous ingot. The idea had come to Oakley during a moment of frustration at having to use two hands to eat her favourite snack, and she felt sure that the bars would, with time and the right investors, become as ubiquitous as their cereal counterparts. She had but a single home-made sample with her, which visitors were welcome to touch whilst she reviewed for them some of the notable advantages that crisps squashed into a bar form enjoyed over those loose in a bag: they were easier to fit into children's lunchboxes, they took up less space in kitchen cupboards and they could be moulded into pine-tree shapes for Christmas and hearts for Valentine's Day. The marketing of the product was the province of Oakley's boyfriend, an intense young man obviously in awe of his partner's talents, who pressured me to bite off a corner of the sample bar and take an information pack home with me. I tried to reflect on what other consumer goods were currently using up valuable

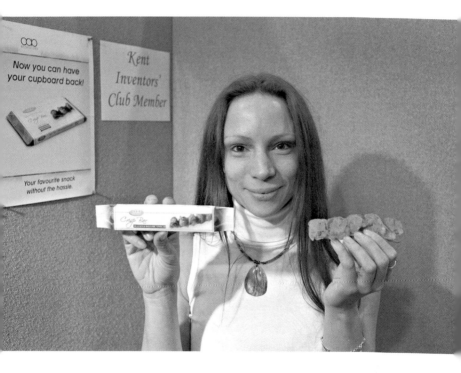

space in air-filled containers and might one day benefit from being compressed into rods, but I lost my train of thought. I moved on to reflect on how the pair behind the Crisp Bar might beat a dignified retreat from this high-point of entrepreneurial energy: how they might fend off the well-meaning and unintentionally humiliating enquiries of neighbours and consider their crisp experience from the vantage point of old age, the sole memento of their venture a box of marketing materials stowed in a corner of the attic next to their children's cast-off playthings.

Entrepreneurship appears to be almost wholly dependent on a sense that the present order is an unreliable and cowardly indicator of the possible. The absence of certain practices and products is deemed by entrepreneurs to be neither right nor inevitable, but merely evidence of the conformity and lack of imagination of the herd. Yet the milieu also demands that its protagonists develop a hard-headed awareness of certain intractable financial and legal truths, as well as an accurate sense of what other human beings are actually like. The field seems to require a painfully uncommon synthesis of imagination and realism.

3.

Given the rarity of this combination, it was particularly ominous to see so many people being encouraged to have a go. The popularity of the fair (as well as its vigorous promotion by a local authority and a government agency) suggested how closely linked the idea of launching a new business is to the modern notion of fulfilment, being filtered through our society via admiring profiles of high-flying entrepreneurs, coupled with a relative silence regarding the bankruptcies and not-infrequent suicides of their less accomplished colleagues. The start-up company may be as central to our contemporary ideals as the ritual of praying for the souls of the dead or the maintenance of female virginity was to the values of our medieval ancestors.

Yet in reality, the likelihood of reaching the pinnacle of capitalist society today is only marginally better than were the chances of being accepted into the French nobility four centuries ago, though at least an aristocratic age was franker, and therefore kinder, about the odds. It did not relentlessly play up the possibilities open to all those with a take on the future of the potato crisp, and so, in turn, did not cruelly equate an ordinary life with a failed one.

Our era is perverse in passing off an exception as a rule. The statistical probabilities of successfully rerouting commercial reality were laid bare for me by a wry venture capitalist who had come to the fair with few expectations, save for having the opportunity to spend a day away from his office. Of the two thousand business plans he received a year, he said, he immediately threw out 1,950, scrutinised fifty more closely and ended up investing in ten. Within five years, out of those ten enterprises, four would be bankrupt, another four would be stuck in what was termed a 'graveyard cycle' of low profits and a mere two would be generating the significant returns which keep his industry afloat. Here was a vision of success guaranteed to disappoint 99.9 percent of its subscribers.

Then again, there was a certain heroic beauty in the exuberant destruction of both capital and hope entailed by the entrepreneurs' activities. Money patiently accumulated through decades of unremarkable work would, in a rush of optimism inspired by a flattering business plan, be handed over to a momentarily convincing chief executive, who would hasten to set the pyre alight in a brief, brilliant and largely inconsequential blaze.

Almost all of the exhibitors at the fair were destined to throw themselves at the cliff face of entrepreneurial achievement and fall flat; for example, people like Paul Nolan, who had come up with a system of tilt-out under-bath shelves on which to store cleaning products and toiletries, or Edward van Noord, a publican from Amsterdam who had devoted his life's savings to the development of 1-2-3 Stop Fire, a disposable fire-extinguishing system with a restricted applicability in the real world – just two of the many participants of the fair who would one day be compelled to return to more modest ways of anchoring the motives for their existence.

Nevertheless, these entrepreneurs could at least be celebrated for embodying an honourably stubborn side of human nature, one which in other areas causes us to get married without duress and to behave as if death might be an avoidable condition. They were proof of the extent to which we ultimately prefer excitement and disaster to boredom and safety.

In the early afternoon, I dropped in on a session of the British Inventors' Society, where one of the members was unveiling an idea for a deodorant-dispensing machine designed to be installed in railway stations – a concept premised on his realisation that he and his fellow commuters were prone to sweat prodigiously on their way to and from crowded city platforms. The society's members were united by their belief that the manner in which the world was presently organised was in no way representative of its full potential. They were in the habit of scanning their homes and environments for anything which did not function optimally: rubbish bags which declined to close securely, lunchboxes which were too hard to clean or parking posts which would have been better off retracting automatically when lorries backed over them. Although I had never invented anything, as the afternoon drew on (and the after-

effects of a few glasses of wine I had ordered over lunch kicked in),
I felt able to share with the group some of my own tentative notions
for businesses as yet missing from the world economy, including
a new kind of holiday company which would take tourists around
industrial locations rather than museums; a chain of secular chapels
which atheists could visit to appease their confused religious yearnings; and restaurants which would focus on offering diners instruction in the arts of friendship and conversation rather than on the
food itself. Even among people as broad-minded as the inventors,
my list precipitated a tense silence.

It has often been said that while any fool can have a good idea,
only a few great minds have it in them to start a profitable business.
The members of the British Inventors' Society seemed to turn this
unflattering equation on its head (pleasingly so in the eyes of a writer,
a species congenitally fated to be better at thinking up ideas than
at knowing what to do with them). These inventors were elevating
the formulation of entrepreneurial ideas to the status of a visionary
activity. Though forced to justify their efforts in the pragmatic language of venture capital, they were at heart utopian thinkers intent
on transforming the world for the better, one deodorant-dispensing
machine at a time.

4.
A series of speakers with claims to entrepreneurial insight had
been invited to address the delegates in the late afternoon. Trevor
Thwaite, a civil servant, gave a lecture entitled, with a levity which
could not quite disguise the anxiety embedded in its theme, 'How
to Turn That Gem of an Idea into Shed-Loads of Money'. Three
people attended, including a Malaysian man who had invented a
portable lightning conductor.

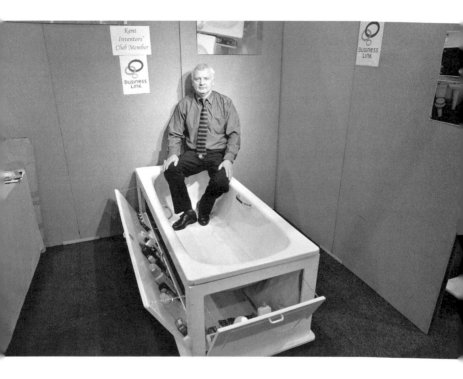

The auditorium was considerably more animated when, to mark the close of proceedings, the fair was graced by the presence of a famous Scottish industrialist almost universally referred to simply as Sir Bob. Over the course of a forty-year career in business, Sir Bob had amassed a billion pounds, a sum he was planning to bequeath in full to the library at Glasgow University, in part so as to teach his two children about the value of money. Sir Bob had begun in bathroom tiles. After recognising, as a precocious sixteen-year-old plumber's apprentice, just how phlegmatic the sector was, he had built up a chain of warehouses offering eight thousand different varieties of tiles, manufactured at a plant in Romania for a fraction of their retail price. These harshly lit emporia, echoing with the sound of managers haranguing customers with news of unmissable discounts, had rung the death knell for every small tile merchant from Aberdeen to St Ives and were inextricably linked in the public mind to the abortive redecorating projects of many an ill-tempered rainy weekend. The next jewel in Sir Bob's crown was a chain of gyms which made the lion's share of its money in the two weeks after New Year's, from people too distracted by their swollen body-mass index to read the small print appended to punitive member-ship schemes. This was followed, fittingly enough, by fifty shops in Scotland and the north of England catering to what Sir Bob called the 'larger lady'. His interests now ranged from health care to finan-cial services. He owned a dozen motorway bridges in Denmark and a cement plant in Albania.

The president of the British Inventors' Society had been assigned the task of introducing Sir Bob to the assembly, but undermined his good intentions by digressing at length about a trip he had lately made to the Balearics and the details of his son's wedding plans, before revealing, at an exceptionally leisurely pace, just how privileged he and his fellow organisers felt to be hosting Sir Bob – who, standing beside him wearing a fixed expression and a pair of platform shoes, was looking less privileged to have accepted the invitation with every new chapter of the interminable encomium.

When at last the time came for Sir Bob, one metre fifty tall, to take the microphone, he sounded closer to anger than the title of his talk – 'The Entrepreneur in All of Us' – might have led his audience to foresee. He fired off an expletive-dotted Scots-cadenced tirade against bureaucrats, red tape, no-gooders, scroungers, trust funders and tax inspectors before turning his attention to the ten things his career had taught him about the art of making money. Regrettably, the list was profoundly platitudinous, either because he wanted to keep the real secrets close to his chest until he was safely entombed, and his money was on its way to Hillhead, or because he genuinely did not know quite how or why he, the son of an unemployed Glasgow dockworker, had succeeded in becoming one of the wealthiest people on the face of the globe – and had hence merely settled on some suggestions of where his talents lay culled from business books picked up at airport newsstands.

Whatever his stated strengths, it appeared that the one area in which Sir Bob excelled was anxiety. He was marked out by his relentless ability to find fault with others' mediocrity – suggesting that a certain kind of intelligence may at heart be nothing more or less than a superior capacity for dissatisfaction. He admitted to a thoroughgoing distrust of all his employees and subcontractors, to an insistence on personally signing off on all expenses accrued within any of his companies and to a habit of staying up for much of every night scrutinising an array of spreadsheets – no doubt long after Edward van Noord of 1-2-3 Stop Fire had slipped into an unvexed sleep in his house in the suburbs of Amsterdam.

We tend to cling to the notion that all human qualities should cohere, that we may be at once beautiful and thoughtful, vigilant and relaxed, gifted and well balanced – but it seemed clear that, admirable though Sir Bob's achievements and energy might be, it would surely not be such a treat to be his wife or son.

At least Sir Bob was inspiringly democratic. In any area of business he happened to contemplate, he refused to believe that success would be impossible for someone like him. His varied activities had furnished him with an unusually keen sense of how things worked, freeing him of the naive and childish perspective from which most of us still see the world. He regarded the large artefacts of finance and industry which surround us, and which we often assume to be as inevitable as the earth's natural features – our warehouses, shopping centres, control towers, banks and holidays resorts – not as the products of remote or obscure processes, but of efforts by people a little like himself, plucky and hard-working types who felt that destiny was theirs to mould. He knew how things fitted together: he knew how to finance a supermarket and go about building a fifty-two-storey skyscraper. He knew which city lawyer could help him to acquire an oil platform and how to negotiate with the government of Australia to buy up private schools in New South Wales. He could look out across any landscape and be confident that it was not the gods who had made it, but people a little like himself. He was – in this sense, at least – a true adult.

There was time allowed for questions after the talk, and a studious-looking man seized the opportunity to stand up and ask why Sir Bob had decided to leave his fortune to a university library. To judge from the latter's monosyllabic response, the inquiry either irritated or bored him. His detachment reminded me of the attitude of the many barons throughout history who had spent their

careers plundering the earth and hounding their employees, but
who then, nearing death, had quietly dropped their loot into foundations which to this day continue to distribute money to impoverished souls afflicted by a strong desire to write monographs on
early Assyrian pottery or to play the bassoon – as if the barons had
ultimately felt they had no other option but to redirect their ambitions and their avarice in order to wind up seeming good in the most
conventional of ways.

5.

I left the entrepreneurial gathering feeling at once inspired and chas
tened. I recognised my admiration for visionaries such as Mohsen
Bahmani (of the floating shoes), whose fledgling businesses sought
to pick up on and exploit desires overlooked by more mainstream
enterprises. Yet I also appreciated the extent to which the aims of
these energetic men and women were undermined by their obvious
misunderstanding of how people actually went about making decisions on such matters as how to cross a lake or eat crisps, how to
store products in the bathroom or put out a fire. These individuals
were writing their stories in a subgenre of contemporary fiction, the
business plan, and populating them with characters endowed with
deeply implausible personalities, an oversight which would eventually be punished not by a scathing review by some bright young
person from the *London Review of Books* but by a lack of custom and
a prompt foreclosure.

By contrast, Sir Bob's grasp of psychology could not be faulted.
He apprehended the public's love of spacious parking-lots and
prominently advertised deals on discounted bathroom furnishings.
He knew how panicked we could be made to feel about the girth
of our thighs but also how greedy we could become upon spotting

a competitively priced sausage (his holding company had just a few years earlier acquired a profitable stake in a Hamburg-based fast-food chain, *Goldene Bratwurst*). Yet for all his understanding of worldly concerns, when it came to fathoming the deeper meaning of his own furious activity, Sir Bob displayed the sort of laziness for which he himself had no patience in others. He appeared to have only a passing interest in the overall purpose of his financial accumulation and evidently did not care to study whether commerce could by itself deliver any of societal benefits he so mockingly relegated to the pious and unmanly field of charity.

Still, an imaginary merger between the best sides of the visionaries and of Sir Bob yielded something resembling a picture of the ideal entrepreneur. In character a judicious fusion of the utopian and the practical, he or she would succeed not only in identifying an important need but also in mastering the challenges of bureaucracy and finance in order to give the resolution of that need an institutional form, and thereby affect others' lives in ways that theory alone could never do.

This ideal was not, in the event, limited to the realm of the imagination: there were a tantalising array of real-life cases in which entrepreneurs had succeeded in founding innovative schools and progressive political groupings, new forms of community and life-enhancing technologies. I knew how deeply I admired them, because any accounts of their exploits that I came across in the media or (even worse) heard from old friends at parties had an exceptional capacity to catapult me into spasms of envy and inadequacy. These enterprising types had not − like me − fled back into their own dreams at the first mention of a sales tax or an employee ledger; they had instead managed to survive the challenges of finance, law and recruitment and, as a result, they had been able to give their flights of fancy a lucrative and consequential dimension. These paragons bore much the same relation to the mere intellectual as a restaurant-owning chef might to a writer of cookery books.

If there is any excuse for making such bathetic confessions of envy in public, it is that my feelings in this context are unlikely to be unique. A striking number of us (that is, we who have yet to become who we are) are apt, in our private moments, to express our understanding of how the world could be altered for the better by picturing to ourselves various businesses we would like to start. In our more self-indulgent moods, we may even entertain detailed musings about what the awning should look like above the shop or how the advertisements for the new service ought to be phrased. These pleasing and all-consuming daydreams appear to spring from those very same aspects of our personalities which led us as children to delight in running a grocery store out of a corner of the kitchen or to open a hotel in a cardboard box in the garden – as though there was some sort of innate and enduring human impulse to lend entrepreneurial form to certain of our deeply held enthusiasms and insights.

I pledged that I would return to the fair one year with some floating shoes of my own.

X

Aviation

1.

During a time when I was finding it hard to write anything and often spent whole days on my bed wondering about the point of my work, I received a phone call from a Slovenian newspaper, which I had never heard of until then, asking if I might want to travel to Paris on their behalf in order to write an article about the airshow at Le Bourget airport, a major biannual event in the aerospace calendar, where manufacturers gather before the world's airlines and air-forces and try to interest them in wheels, radars, missiles and cabin curtains.

The editor hoped that I might be able to convey to his readers, some one hundred thousand people in Ljubljana and its surrounding hills, what he termed 'the ecstasies of flight' and encouraged me to keep an eye out for any technological breakthroughs which might be poised to transform aviation ('Showers in the sky?' he suggested by way of an example). Though he apologised for a meagre fee and accommodation in a budget hotel overlooking a motorway into Paris, he added that he had passes to many important press conferences, including one at which a member of the royal family of Abu Dhabi, Sheikh Ahmed Bin Saif Al Nahyan, was scheduled to announce an order for twenty-two A380s, with which he planned to cement his emirate into a pre-eminent place on the duty-free map of the globe.

Because the fair was, at least in its first couple of days, tightly restricted to aerospace professionals and the press, it had an atmosphere of calm and easy conviviality, of the kind one might find between guests at a wedding. It was not uncommon to chat to people in the queue for bottled water or, above the sound of a G550 spy-plane pirouetting around the skies of the Ile-de-France, to strike up a conversation with a stranger eating a *pain au chocolat* on an adjoining

seat, thereby opening one's eyes to new horizons, for example, to the tenor of life as a colonel in the airforce of Gabon.

The exhibition halls next to the runway had been divided up by country, which revealed national tempers as these were articulated in aircraft parts. The Swiss specialised in flight instruments, the Brazilians were pre-eminent in propellers and the Ukrainians were attempting, against many odds, to establish themselves in landing gears and metal alloys.

Although the goods on sale were uncommonly expensive, customers shopping for aircraft equipment were presumed not to be impervious to the techniques of the high street and hence to the appeal of a former Miss Sweden dressed in a catsuit, or the lure of a raffle for a free weekend at Euro Disney. At lunchtime, many companies cleared space on their stands to serve up food from their regions, in the hope that a prospective buyer who had decided against a mid-air refuelling tanker from Galicia might glance more favourably upon it in the wake of some slices of dry-cured ham. The representatives of a factory from the foot of the Urals had brought with them a large, linen-wrapped cheese which they carved with a penknife into small cubes, arranging them around the pedestal of a flag of the Russian Federation to inspire goodwill towards the enterprise's chief offering: wheel braces for military cargo aircraft.

Pathos naturally gathered around some of the less frequented stands. It was evident that in no part of the aerospace industry could one be certain of escaping from ruinous competition. Even extreme specialisation – in anti-oxidation systems for wing flaps, for example – carried little guarantee of immunity from rival suitors. There seemed to be no item in the world that five alternative manufacturers had not already simultaneously embarked upon producing. Nevertheless, the bankrupt nature of a business was not always

a sufficient argument against it. High up in the Saudi Arabian government, a decision had been taken to reserve a stand representing the nation's aerospace industry, notwithstanding that no such thing could, in fairness, have been said actually to exist. Twice the size of a normal stall, the Saudi showcase boasted chandeliers, leather sofas and walls wrapped in a sandy felt evocative of the colours of the Taif Mountains. But because there was little for him to discuss, the manager mostly sat by himself, dressed in a maroon suit and tie, silently surveying a stainless-steel platter of dates. To have omitted to come to Paris would have been tantamount to admitting that Saudi Arabia did not build planes, hence that it was uninterested in technological innovation and had abandoned any claim to be counted among forward-looking nations. And yet to have attended, and in such style, only offered surreptitious confirmation of the very problem to which the stand had been proposed as the daring answer.

The displays manned by Russia and its sister states tackled their difficulties with greater vigour. Aeronautical purchases which further west would have required compliance with drawn-out bureaucratic regulations were here sanguinely waved through. It was possible to make an immediate downpayment on a missile system or a Soviet-era satellite, items frequently promoted with the help of short films, perhaps representing a manager's first efforts at cinematography, and which showed machines blasting into the air to the accompaniment of a muscular American-inflected commentary. After being ignored for so long, the arts of salesmanship were now practised with unusual alacrity by people who had assiduously read translations of *The Seven Habits of Highly Effective People*. Unfortunately, as in so much of the consumer world, recognisable brand names were an essential means of providing reassurance, an issue which the Volga

Advanced Passenger Aircraft Company appeared to be finding no easy way to circumvent.

In search of technological breakthroughs, I made my way to a display touting a Japanese manufacturer's new seventy-seat commuter plane, which promised significantly lowered operating costs thanks to certain improvements, whose precise nature was hard to grasp, in its wing design. A full-scale replica of the interior had been shipped to Paris in crates from Yokohama and could be toured by appointment. After an exchange of business cards, I was led inside by two diffident men, in charge of sales and marketing, who locked the door of the quasi-jet behind me, took seats on either side of the aisle and stared mutely ahead towards an imaginary cockpit. I hoped that through some piece of funfair trickery, the machine might now seem to fly, but it appeared that the visit (which good manners dictated would have to last a while) was to have no particular theme or focus, being designed solely to allow customers to examine the seat fittings and the galley – on whose quality I dutifully complimented my hosts, as if they had made them themselves. With the door closed, the noise of the fair had died away, causing the three of us to become uncomfortably aware of the difficulties of human communication. I began to imagine that we had in fact left the outskirts of Paris and were journeying through a part of the stratosphere informed by the purple light which washed in through the windows from the adjoining Pratt & Whitney stand. After an age, the door was reopened, we made our way out and the head of marketing handed me a set of postcards of the plane, adding that he looked forward to meeting me again – though I sensed an atmosphere of melancholy around the enterprise which made me question whether the company would ever succeed in achieving its desired supremacy in the medium-sized regional jet market.

At the stand of the world's second-largest engine manufacturer, I spent some minutes observing an unusually attractive young saleswoman with shoulder-length chestnut hair, dressed in a beige suit, who was biting the nail of her left index finger and crossing her slender legs whilst leaning against a large fan blade. She was not the first of her type I had seen that day, but something about her appearance left me thoughtful. I had until then believed that the vendors' frequent and deliberate reliance on feminine appeal was merely a vulgar stratagem intended to win over airline executives, through an implicit suggestion that a purchase might bring them closer to intimacy with a sales agent. Now I began to see the matter differently: it seemed obvious that no order, however lucrative, would actually render these women available to buyers, so their presence on the stands took on a more poignant and commercially effective dimension. Their real function was to serve as a reminder of the unavailability of beauty to an overwhelmingly male, middle-aged and harried-looking base of customers. The women were goading the men to lay aside all romantic ambitions and to focus instead on their business and technological agendas. Rather than seductresses, they were in truth spurs to sublimation, and symbols of everything that the buyers would be better off if they forgot about in order to concentrate on the thousands of pieces of precisely engineered equipment arranged around the halls.

For my part, led on by the priorities of the Slovenian newspaper, I went to a few press conferences. There was almost always an initial problem with the microphone. Men sat at tables decorated with the flags of their respective companies and announced deals before handfuls of journalists. It was often difficult to discover what the significance of these agreements might be, for they were framed in a language of acronyms that repelled the curiosity of minds

nourished on the undemanding fare of the ordinary press. I read in *Flight Daily News* that UPS had chosen ADS-B for their next generation avionics, while *Aviation International* reported that Klimov was putting a VK800 against the P&WC PT6. The obscurity of these events, on which depended the livelihoods of many in factories across continents, only served to underline the marginality of the stories normally found in the daily paper, which has no option but to focus on murders, divorces and films, for its readers cannot be expected to follow in detail any of the real developments which unfold obscurely in the realms of science and economics and on which our future depends.

Many countries had sent military delegations to survey and order new equipment. On the way to the fair from the hotel, it was not uncommon to encounter a high-ranking member of one of the world's poorer airforces sitting on a commuter train, his row of medals hinting at martial achievements far removed from the routines of his fellow passengers bound for the office. It was on just such a train on the last morning of the airshow that I began chatting with three representatives of a central Asian republic. Each of them was carrying a small bag, containing a towel and a change of underwear, because their hotel, which forced me to re-evaluate the merits of my own, had a broken boiler and the airmen had heard that there were shower facilities in the exhibition halls.

They were principally interested in twin-engine strike aircraft. Though they could not lay claim to the sums required for a Typhoon Eurofighter, they nevertheless approached its manufacturer with the confidence of well-seasoned negotiators, their haughtiness implying that they would have no trouble finding a range of alternative delta-winged machines elsewhere if suitable terms could not be agreed.

The Eurofighter salesman led them up a small ladder to the cockpit. There seemed to be a struggle for leadership among the men and some harsh-sounding words were exchanged before they worked out the order in which they would have their turns at the controls, while each of those left waiting looked on suspiciously at his two colleagues, alert for any signs of unfavourable treatment. Through the glass canopy, the view across the runway was of a row of small terraced houses, many with washing hanging on the line. But when my new friends took the joystick, their eyes appeared to be somewhere else entirely, perhaps imagining the aircraft at Mach 2 over the Pamir Mountains heading down along the Fedchenko Glacier, after unloading on their enemy a battery of Storm Shadow air to ground missiles, thereby putting behind them the humiliations of former conflicts, with freezing nights in caves and the smell of camels' breath in the dewy dawn.

Towards the close of the fair's final afternoon session, I learnt that Sheikh Ahmed Bin Saif Al Nahyan had cancelled his visit due to the illness of a favourite falcon, and would instead put out a press release outlining the main points of his $22 billion purchase. Wishing to delay for as long as possible my return to an empty hotel room, I wandered through the Airbus stand, inspecting see-through model fuselages of yet-to-be-built aeroplanes, admiring the meticulous rows of miniature seats arranged inside and reflecting on the ambitious plans in the works for the future of business class. Now that most of the delegates had left, cleaning crews arrived and set about wiping fingerprints off engines and rearranging brochures on countertops. The insistent hum of their vacuum cleaners seemed to call into question the significance of what was referred to by its manufacturer as the Airbus family, and for the first time in days, I found myself thinking of something other than aviation.

I should not have worried about my evening, for when I got back to my hotel, I discovered that a closing-night celebration was in progress. Realising that the majority of their guests were connected to the fair, the management had seen an opportunity to raise additional revenue by throwing a pay-as-you-go party at the bar. Here was my chance to meet in the flesh people whom I had over the previous few days been able only to imagine on the bases of the whirring sounds made by their toilet-roll dispensers, and their sides of mobile-phone conversations, as heard through the thin and even bendy walls which separated us. The hotel did not seem to have been housing anyone in a position either to buy or sell a plane: such dignitaries were more likely to have booked into the Crillon in central Paris, and at that moment were perhaps sailing around the Ile de la Cité on the Boeing-sponsored dinner cruise, searching for appropriate remarks to make about the illuminated flying buttresses of Notre Dame, first built by stonemasons in the 1240s. By contrast, this place was the preferred lodging for those known within the industry as Tier 3 or 4 suppliers, people involved in the manufacture of smaller and less sophisticated parts of aircraft, or indeed, even further from the end product, in the fabrication of the tools required to form these parts.

Over an Orangina-based cocktail, I made the acquaintance of a salesman from Fort Worth, Texas. His company produced the rubber hoses responsible for circulating oxygen, fuel and oil around commercial jets. With unintended lyricism, he described to me how these prosthetic veins sent their liquids coursing under passengers' seats as they soared obliviously over cloud-covered seas towards their objectives. Sensing my interest, he bent down and pulled out of his oversized accountant's briefcase a brochure showing three grey warehouses with red stripes across their rooflines, located on an industrial estate near Dallas–Fort Worth airport. 'No other company can equal our track record of providing horizontal, integrated fuel solutions', the document declared – though the sales director's choice of hotel seemed proof that not every potential client had been prepared to second this buoyant assessment.

Despite the fact that the occasion marked the end of a few days of hard work, many of the partygoers were feeling anxious, whether about orders, stock levels, Civil Aviation Authority regulations or the skittish exchange rate of the dollar. There was particular distress at the news that Northrop Grumman was planning to revamp its procurement process. A man whose business specialised in corrosion checks shared with me his suspicion that he and his wife had chosen the very worst time to renovate their home near Cheyenne, Wyoming, a place name that inanely evoked for me an image of an archetypal log cabin, like the one I had once recently seen in an outsize canvas by the nineteenth-century American landscape painter Thomas Cole.

Troublingly, there was no substantial food to be had, so that as we talked, my interlocutor and I were forced to rely to an unwise degree on crisps and salted nuts. We also made some inroads on the cocktail menu, being conscious that we were not going to be able to solve all our problems that night and surmising that we might, therefore, be better off attempting to lose track of them for a few hours with chemical assistance.

On my way back to our table from the bar, carrying a third round, I was struck by what seemed like a profound realisation that the air show was only one of hundreds of industry-specific events taking place at that moment around the world, filling airport concourses with delegates, providing custom for the makers of rolling suitcases, giving life to motorway-side motels and supporting careers in the pornographic film industry. There were conventions devoted to seaside condos and dental equipment, waste management and pharmaceuticals, weddings and caravans. And behind these fairs, there were confirmation faxes being sent to Sheratons and Best Westerns, and room-service trays, some decorated with sliced pickles, wending their way from kitchens to guest rooms down the lugubrious passageways of Crowne Plazas and Fairfield Inns & Suites.

A disco ball started spinning, and along with it ABBA. Because it had been a long day and it was unlikely that any of us would ever meet again, it did not seem inappropriate to dance, especially when the speakers began throbbing to 'Super Trouper', a song whose obscure lyrics hinted at an international liaison facilitated by the very planes that had inspired our gathering.

The delegates danced to forget the anxieties of salesmanship and to shake off the nervous anticipation generated by industry gossip. They danced to stop thinking about the dynamic future of aviation, with its next generation of afterburners and electromechanical flight decks, its promises of low-fuel-burning engines and nanotechnological wings. With the help of the disco ball, we managed to restore ourselves to the imperfect present, as constituted by a dimly lit bar next to a motorway somewhere in the midst of an industrial cityscape of factories and convention centres. We held one another's moist palms and swayed across the tiled floor, gaining relief through our shared humanity – our stomachs bloated from too many nuts, our waistlines expanding, our digestions unhealthy, our sleep interrupted, our expenses fiddled – creatures who occasionally looked up at the stars but remained essentially and defiantly earthbound.

2.

The experience of the air show stayed with me. I began to think differently about planes. When airborne, I assessed the seat upholstery, the ailerons and the light fittings and dwelt on what their inclusion on board presupposed: exchanges of business cards, grey warehouses, salesmen's suitcases and cubes of cheese arranged on plates at convention stands. I no longer regarded the plastic casing around the windows as either inevitable or natural, but as the patiently refined result of a manufacturing process once agreed upon by two men on a podium with flags in front of them, captured by a photographer from *Flight Daily News*.

Half a year later, I was invited to give a lecture at California State University in Bakersfield, a two-hour drive north of where I was staying in Los Angeles. It was my intention to complete the round trip in a day, but as I headed out of Bakersfield in the middle of the afternoon – after a lecture notable for its near-unanimous absence of attendees – I took a wrong exit, onto a divided motorway which funnelled me irrevocably in a south-easterly direction, into the Mojave Desert.

Signs of civilisation rapidly disappeared, ceding the field to a ceaseless repetition of barren lunar valleys – though to suggest that this landscape looked like the moon was unfairly to deflect responsibility for a bleakness which was patently not our neighbouring planet's alone. Vultures circled overhead. Occasionally, after a few miles of terrain unaltered since the end of the last ice age, there would be renewed evidence of man's presence, and hence a fresh opportunity to wonder at our species' strangeness, especially our inclination to put up billboards even in the most desolate areas that read, 'Great Fahitas, Low Prices'. There were scattered ruins, too: stone cabins missing their roofs and windows, crumbling slowly back into the desert, looking so ancient that it seemed inconceivable they could have been put up by gold prospectors only in the 1880s, rather than by group of itinerant Roman legionnaires some centuries before the birth of Christ.

After an hour or two of driving in circles, furious at my own ineptitude, I surrendered hope of making it back to Los Angeles that day and pulled in at a motel in the small town of Mojave. In a sombre hallway, following a few introductory remarks about the weather, Kimberly offered me a choice of a deluxe room overlooking the swimming pool or a cheaper, regular room over the car park, adding that I might prefer the latter   on account of the train.

There was no time for elaboration before, with melodramatic suddenness, a roar presently engulfed the hotel, negating all possibility of speech for the next four minutes. The sound reverberated around the valley, echoing off the cliff faces of the Tehachapi Mountains and making manifest the vastness of the sandy bowl in which the town lay. Mojave was positioned across one of the country's most congested rail junctions. Freight trains, many of them a hundred cars long, came through day and night bearing chemicals and aggregates, canned fruits and television sets, cattle carcasses and corn flour. The trains were on their way north and east, from the port at Long Beach to depots in Denver and Chicago, and were so heavily loaded that despite being pushed along by as many as eight separate locomotives apiece, rarely achieved speeds of more than fifty kilometres an hour. On cloudy nights, in the canyons between Mojave and Bakersfield, gangs of Mexican thieves often succeeded in jumping onto these ponderous trains and cutting open containers of valuable cargo. Every month, one or two of their number would be found dead on the desert floor, surrounded by bin bags full of running shoes from Vietnam, having lost their way among the rocks and crevasses. Kimberly showed me an account of just such a mis-adventure which had been published in the local paper. Decidedly unmoved and vengeful in tone, it appeared to be squarely on the side of the shoes.

The experience of the train made it hard to leave. Learning of it was akin to having seduced someone in a bar only to discover, when she stood up to dance or go to the bathroom, that she had only one leg. I secured a key from Kimberly and headed to my room, from which I almost immediately realised I would have to escape until the instant when I felt ready to go to sleep. I headed back downstairs to take advantage of the swimming pool. A teenaged girl was sitting next to it on a sun lounger and cutting her toenails, which rico-cheted remarkable distances across a turquoise-coloured concrete floor. Unfortunately, most of the budget for the pool had apparently been squandered on proclaiming – in an enormous illuminated display by the roadside – that it existed, leaving few resources for it actually to do so. It was the minimum size to qualify as a pool before it would have to be recategorised as a bath.

I went back to the car for a drive around Mojave. However, like many small towns in the American west, it seemed not to have a centre where citizens could gather for fellowship, javelin contests and philosophical debate, as they had done, according to most his-torical accounts, in Athens in the age of Pericles. There was not even a Wal-Mart. Judging by the number of signs devoted to it, the main attraction was the airport, which ran diagonally across the town and comprised a few huts, a hangar, two Cessnas and a landing strip. In the pale late-afternoon sky, an ultralight aircraft was advanc-ing slowly over the valley, making no discernible progress. But as I continued around the airfield, a more arresting spectacle came into view: on the horizon at the far end of the runway, the entire aeronautical population of a sizeable international airport appeared to have touched down and been parked in close formation, wing tip to wing tip, as if a calamity I had not yet heard about had prompted a mass migration by aircraft from every continent to this particular corner of southern California. There were representatives from the Netherlands, Australia, South Korea, Zimbabwe and Switzerland; there were short-haul Airbuses and giant 747s. Adding to the eeriness of the scene, the planes had none of their usual supporting equipment – no jetties, buses, baggage carts or refuelling trucks. They sat unattended in the desert shrub, their passengers seemingly still waiting inside for the doors to be opened.

Only when I got nearer to them did I apprehend that each of the planes had suffered a particular injury. Several were missing their noses; others had their intakes and sensor probes wrapped in silver foil; a few had lost their undercarriages and were being held up off the ground by packing crates. An Air India 737 had been sliced in half and dug into the sand, so that its cockpit pointed up towards the sky, with no sign of its rear fuselage.

The aircraft were cordoned off by a barbed-wire fence, to one side of which was a rudimentary single-storey administrative building. Hoping to secure permission to take a closer look, I pushed open a corrugated steel door and found myself in the middle of an office. The occupant was squatting beneath his desk, dealing with a printer problem which had sunk him into the sort of cataclysmically sour mood that typically accompanies such a predicament. 'No,' he shouted at me, without even raising his head. I explained that I had been driving by the airfield and had been captivated by the peculiar and desolate beauty of the gigantic machines which lay abandoned, and slowly decomposing, in the desert.

'Fuck off, we don't give tours,' he responded decisively.

Certain that his logic would benefit from being exposed to the deeper wellspring of my curiosity, I proceeded to deliver a soliloquy, a polished but approximate version of which it seems unfair to deprive the reader:

'My desire further to investigate these semi-ruined objects, though personal in nature, nevertheless fits into a long Western tradition of preoccupation with the remnants of collapsing civilisations, which can be traced at least as far back as the eighteenth century. It was then that large numbers of ruin-gazers, Goethe among them, travelled to the Italian peninsula to admire the remains of ancient Rome, often by moonlight, deriving solace from the sight of once-grand palaces and theatres now covered in weeds and sheltering wolves and wild dogs. The Germans, always a proficient people in the coining of compound words, invented the term *Ruinenlust* to describe this new passion. It seems, in fact, that the more advanced a society is, the greater will be its interest in ruined things, for it will see in them a redemptively sobering reminder of the fragility of its own achievements. Ruins pose a direct challenge to our concern with power and rank, with bustle and fame. They puncture the inflated folly of our exhaustive and frenetic pursuit of wealth. It stands to reason, therefore, that a visitor to the United States, this most technologically developed of all modern societies, should take a particular interest in the flip side of the nation's progress. The disintegrating Continental Airlines 747 visible outside of your window seems the equivalent, for myself, of what the Coliseum in Rome must have been for the young Edward Gibbon.'

There was a silence as my companion took in the eloquence, cultural range and sheer profundity of what I had just said. The buzz of the ultralight could still be heard high overhead. But the man was evidently disinclined by nature to pay extravagant compliments, for when he finally spoke, it was to say 'Fuck off' again with a resolve which his previous riposte had perhaps lacked – to which sentiment he then added, lest there remain any ambiguity, 'Get the hell out of here before I shoot you in the ass.'

Fortunately, the man was not as unreasonable as this might have implied. He had a fine understanding of the value of money and a few twenty-dollar bills later, we had agreed that I would be free to wander around the site until he closed it at nightfall, though I would first have to sign a lengthy legal document guaranteeing that I (or in the event of my death, my relatives) would never attempt to sue him or his heirs for any injuries that I might incur due to the many dangers outside, which included but were not limited to razor-sharp pieces of severed aircraft wings, unstable fuselages and the triangular-headed Mojave rattlesnakes who made their homes amidst the planes' galleys, engines and seats. My mentor saw me off with a surprisingly gentle word of warning about the desert tortoises who also roamed amongst the wreckage. Many were over a hundred years old, he said – putting them well into their twenties or thirties by the time the *Spirit of Saint Louis* conquered the Atlantic – but were wary of strangers and apt to release their bladders if surprised, thereby losing their whole season's water supply, on which their survival depended.

Out on the airfield, the damage was greater than I had imagined. While a few of the planes were still whole, most had already been so extensively gutted and filleted for spare parts that only their rib cages were left intact. The ground was strewn with undercarriages and engines, seats and cargo boxes, ailerons and elevators. Machines which had spent the better part of their working lives being cosseted by engineers and highly trained mechanics had in death been hacked at with chain saws and diggers.

It was surprisingly noisy too. Food-trolley doors, seat belts and upended toilet seats clacked in the wind, making the place sound like a marina in a storm. Many of the planes wore liveries testifying to corporate hubris: Midway, Braniff, Novair, African Air Express, TWA, Swissair. Most had started out in the fleets of well-funded flag carriers and then over time had slipped down the rungs of the aviation ladder until, in their final employment, they were reduced to doing midnight cargo runs from Miami to San Juan and back or shuttling between Addis Ababa and Harare, their once-immaculate first-class seats patched up with silver duct tape.

One Somali Airlines 707 was lying on its side, with only one wing still attached. Qantas had bought the machine in 1966 and flown it between London and Sydney for eight years before selling it on to Malaysian Airlines. In Kuala Lumpur, the new owners had exchanged the kangaroo painted on its tail for a stylised bird and removed the first-class compartment. After completing a decade's worth of trips to Hong Kong, the plane – by now badly stained around the rear of its fuselage – had been passed on to the Somalis. Limping aloft with the help of unauthorised spare parts, the Boeing had ferried soldiers, smugglers, aid workers and tourists between Mogadishu, Johannesburg and Frankfurt. Then had come an accident with a van at Mogadishu airport, a bullet wound in the tail during a battle with insurgents and an emergency landing in Nairobi with one of the engines on fire. After the airline went broke and its CEO was shot dead in a bungled robbery, an agreement was reached to ship the frail machine to its last resting place.

It was striking to see how quickly the planes had aged: though the oldest of these examples had not yet been off the production line for half a century, they seemed more antique than a Greek temple. Inside the cabins were remnants of now-obsolete technologies:

outsize Bakelite phones, coils of fat electric cables, bulky boxes on the ceilings where film projectors had once been slotted. The cockpits had seats for flight engineers, whose jobs were presently being done by computers the size of hardcover books. Some aircraft still sported their Pratt & Whitney JT3D engines, the proud workhorses of the 1970s, which had generated a then-remarkable 17,500 pounds of thrust, little guessing that a few decades later their successors would, with a fraction of the fuel or noise output, be capable of producing five times that.

What makes the prospect of death distinctive in the modern age is the background of permanent technological and sociological revolution against which it is set, and which serves to strip us of any possible faith in the permanence of our labours. Our ancestors could believe that their achievements had a chance of bearing up against the flow of events. We know time to be a hurricane. Our buildings, our sense of style, our ideas, all of these will soon enough be anachronisms, and the machines in which we now take inordinate pride will seem no less bathetic than Yorick's skull.

Identifying a TWA plane which had lost both its cockpit and its wheels, I climbed up into the fuselage and arranged myself in seat 1C, a royal-blue executive chair with a large stain in the middle of its lower cushion. It was seven in the evening but still bright and agreeably warm. I wanted to press the call button and order a Coke from the stewardess, who was perhaps now dead. I noticed that a few rows behind me, the emergency oxygen masks had dropped down from the overhead compartment. They had done so not in the gruesome accident one associates them with, when the engines are on fire and the emergency slide lies tumescent around the main door, the ladies having grown too troubled to remember to remove their high-heeled shoes, but simply through the slow erosion of their

spring catches. Perhaps we are always more likely to die like this, without particular drama, without firemen in smoke hoods and foam on the runway, without the comfort of a collective accident and the sympathy of newscasters, but through an insipidly slow process of disintegration, the masks only gradually wearing loose and swinging idly in the desert wind, witnessed by rattlesnakes and shy and incontinent desert tortoises.

My thoughts turned to the people who had built and animated these machines, the employees who had exchanged business cards at Le Bourget at the Paris air show of 1968, who had made the Bakelite intercom phones in Trenton, New Jersey, followed the expansion of Eastern Airlines and, in a factory near Calgary, fashioned the blankets which were now disappearing into the Mojave dust. I thought, too, of the captain, and of the flirtatious remarks he might have exchanged with the stewardess who brought his dinner in to him on a tin-foil-covered tray during a trip down to the Caribbean in 1971, the same year Idi Amin came to power and John Newcombe won his third Wimbledon. I imagined his gold braided cap and his aviator glasses, his tanned, bristly arms, his descent towards the tarmac at Kingston and his purple and magenta room overlooking the pool of the newly opened Sunseeker Club near the airport.

How improbable the thought of his own death would have seemed to him, how contrary to his aerobic body and acute mind. There would have been few reminders or signs that there were a finite number of times that his knees would comfortably bend to pick up a suitcase, that eventually even his most basic thoughts would become too arduous for him to connect, that he was working his way through the ten thousand days still allocated to him and that the small daily jolts of anxiety he experienced when dealing with congestion at O'Hare or bad weather over the Gulf of Mexico would one morning reach critical mass in the form of a sudden and definitive tightening in the chest in a driveway in a Phoenix suburb.

Death is hard to keep in mind when there is work to be done: it seems not so much taboo as unlikely. Work does not by its nature permit us to do anything other than take it too seriously. It must destroy our sense of perspective, and we should be grateful to it for precisely that reason, for allowing us to mingle ourselves promiscuously with events, for letting us wear thoughts of our own death and the destruction of our enterprises with beautiful lightness, as mere intellectual propositions, while we travel to Paris to sell engine oil. We function on the basis of a necessary myopia. Therein is the sheer energy of existence, a blind will no less impressive than that which we find in a moth arduously crossing a window ledge, stepping around a dollop of paint left by a too-hasty brush, refusing to contemplate the broader scheme in which he will be dead by nightfall.

The arguments for our triviality and vulnerability are too obvious, too well known and too tedious to rehearse. What is interesting is that we may take it upon ourselves to approach tasks with utter determination and gravity even when their wider non-sense is clear. The impulse to exaggerate the significance of what we are doing, far from being an intellectual error, is really life itself coursing through us. Good health encourages us to identify with all human experiences in all lands, to sigh at a murder in a faraway country, to hope for economic growth and technological progress far beyond the limits of our own lifespan, forgetting that we are never more than a few rogue cells away from the end.

To see ourselves as the centre of the universe and the present time as the summit of history, to view our upcoming meetings as being of overwhelming significance, to neglect the lessons of cemeteries, to read only sparingly, to feel the pressure of deadlines, to

snap at colleagues, to make our way through conference agendas marked '11:00 a.m. to 11:15 a.m.: coffee break', to behave heedlessly and greedily and then to combust in battle – maybe all of this, in the end, is working wisdom. It is paying death too much respect to prepare for it with sage prescriptions. Let it surprise us while we are shipping wood pulp across the Baltic Sea, removing the heads of tuna, developing a nauseating variety of biscuit, advising a client on a change of career, firing a satellite with which to beguile a genera-tion of Japanese schoolgirls, painting an oak tree in a field, laying an electricity line, doing the accounts, inventing a deodorant dispenser or making an extended-strength coiled tube for an airliner. Let death find us as we are building up our matchstick protests against its waves.

If we could witness the eventual fate of every one of our projects, we would have no choice but to succumb to immediate paralysis. Would anyone who watched the departure of Xerxes' army on its way to conquer the Greeks, or Taj Chan Ahk giving orders for the construction of the golden temples of Cancuén, or the British colo-nial administrators inaugurating the Indian postal system, have had it in their hearts to fill their passionate actors in on the eventual fate of their efforts?

Our work will at least have distracted us, it will have provided a perfect bubble in which to invest our hopes for perfection, it will have focused our immeasurable anxieties on a few relatively small-scale and achievable goals, it will have given us a sense of mastery, it will have made us respectably tired, it will have put food on the table. It will have kept us out of greater trouble.

Picture Acknowledgements

This project was designed as much as a photo reportage as an essay. I had the privilege of working from the outset with the photographer Richard Baker (www.bakerpictures.com), to whom I owe a great debt, both for his eye and for his unflagging good humour in moments of crisis. A fuller selection of images can be seen at: www. alaindebotton.com/work

Additional picture credits: Chapter Three: Edward Hopper, *New York Movie*, © Museum of Modern Art, New York. Chapter Six: Images of Stephen Taylor © Ken Adlard, New Moon Photography, Norfolk; aerial photograph of the tree, Stephen Taylor (www. stephentaylorpaintings.com), courtesy Essex and Suffolk Gliding Club; photograph of gallery interior, Vertigo, 62 Great Eastern Street, London, courtesy of the artist.

Acknowledgements

I am grateful to the many institutions and individuals who allowed me access to their places of work and spent many hours discussing their occupations with me. Particular thanks are due to Martin Garside, Glenys Dawson, Fred Stroyan, Lucy Pelham Burn, Mariyam Seena, Sarah Mahir, Yasir Waheed, Mamduh W., Naleem Mohamed, Salma Ahmed, Ibrahim Rayan, Franco Bonacina, Jose Rossi, Brigitte Kolmsee, Jason Orton, Iain McAulay. Some names have been altered in the text to protect identities. I would also like to thank Tom Weldon, Helen Fraser, John Makinson, Dorothy Straight, Joana Niemeyer, Dan Frank, Nicole Aragi, Simon Prosser, Caroline Dawnay and Charlotte de Botton. I am grateful to Faber & Faber and Random House, New York, for permission to quote from W. H. Auden's poem 'The Managers' in Chapter Eight.

Also available in Penguin Paperback

The Consolations of Philosophy

Alain de Botton has set six of the finest minds in the history of philosophy to work on the problems of everyday life. Here then are Socrates, Epicurus, Seneca, Montaigne, Schopenhauer and Nietzsche on some of the things that bother us all: lack of money, the pain of love, inadequacy, anxiety, the fear of failure and the pressure to conform.

'Few discussions on the great philosophers can have been so entertaining ... an ingenious and intelligent book' *Sunday Times*

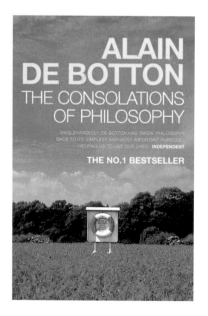

The Art of Travel

The perfect antidote to those guides that tell us what to do when we get there, *The Art of Travel* tries to explain why we really went in the first place – and helpfully suggests how we might be happier on our journeys.

'Lucid, fluid, uplifting … it can enrich and improve your life'
Sunday Times

Status Anxiety

We all worry about what others think of us. We all long to succeed and fear failure. We all suffer – to a greater or lesser degree, usually privately and with embarrassment – from status anxiety. For the first time, Alain de Botton gives a name to this universal condition and sets out to investigate both its origins and its solutions.

'De Botton's gift is to prompt us to think about how we live and how we might change things' *The Times*

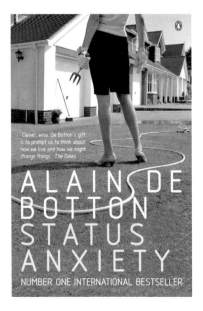

The Architecture of Happiness

The Architecture of Happiness will take you on a beguiling tour through the history and psychology of architecture and interior design, and will for ever alter your relationship with buildings. It will change the way you look at your current home – and help you make the right decisions about your next one.

'Full of splendid ideas, happily and beautifully expressed' *Independent*